NATIONAL
SECURITY
THROUGH
CIVILIAN-BASED
DEFENSE

NATIONAL SECURITY THROUGH CIVILIAN-BASED DEFENSE

Gene Sharp

Professor of Political Science and Sociology
Southeastern Massachusetts University

Program on Nonviolent Sanctions
in Conflict and Defense
Center for International Affairs
Harvard University

Association for Transarmament Studies
Omaha, Nebraska

ISBN 0-9614256-0-1

Library of Congress Cataloging-in-Publication Data

Sharp, Gene.
    National security through civilian-based defense.

    Bibliography: p.
    1. National security. 2. Passive resistance.
I. Title. II. Title: Civilian-based defense.
UA10.5.S52 1985   355'.03   85-15043
ISBN 0-9614256-0-1 (pbk.)

Association for Transarmament Studies
3636 Lafayette Avenue
Omaha, Nebraska 68131
(402) 558-2085

CONTENTS

PREFACE

Many people are now convinced that we need alternatives to present military deterrence and defense policies. The alternatives are usually still sought within the context of military assumptions and means, and so far only rarely beyond them. The search for alternatives is important and needs to be intensified. Present policies, with their serious limitations, would retain few supporters if superior substitute policies existed and were widely known.

Therefore, rather than dissipating our energies arguing about the merits and demerits of present and impending policies, or about the moral adequacy of just war and pacifist positions, we ought to focus primarily on developing effective alternatives and spreading public awareness of them.

This booklet is about one such alternative: *civilian-based defense,* that is, national defense against internal usurpations and foreign invasions by prepared nonviolent noncooperation and defiance by the population and the society's institutions. The aim is to become able to deny attackers their objectives, to become politically unrulable by would-be tyrants, and to subvert the attackers' troops and functionaries to unreliability and even mutiny. Such a prepared capacity, accurately perceived, would provide a different type of deterrent: facing such defense capacity, rational would-be aggressors would choose to stay away!

This policy has reached the level of governmental studies in several European countries. In North America it is receiving growing attention.

Civilian-based defense is not a panacea, nor a doctrine for which believers are sought. We all need to think for ourselves about its application, problems, and potential. We need to suggest to others, if we agree, that it merits investigation. On the basis of greater knowledge and understanding, the policy might be rejected as ineffective or inapplicable. It might, however, be found to provide the basic capacity to enable us to solve both the problems of aggression and of war.

This booklet has been prepared in response to expressions of need for such a brief publication on alternative defense conveyed to me during lecture trips in various parts of the country, from Maine to New Mexico. This booklet is only an introduction to civilian-based defense. Persons who find this of interest are strongly urged to study also the publications recommended for further reading. A newsletter and other educational projects on the policy are being undertaken by the Association for Transarmament Studies, 3636 Lafayette Avenue, Omaha, Nebraska 68131.

The main essay of this booklet was originally published in *War/Peace Report* (New York), April 1970, and was included in my *Exploring Nonviolent Alternatives* (Boston: Porter Sargent Publishers, 1970). The original title was "National Defense Without Armaments." The essay has largely stood the test of time, and has needed only the addition of several substantive discussions and slight editing for this edition.

"Research Areas and Policy Studies on Civilian-based Defense" is a further revision of two previously published papers on the topic: (1) "Research Areas on the Nature, Problems and Potentialities of Civilian Defense" in S.C. Biswas, editor, *Gandhi: Theory and Practice, Social Impact and Contemporary Relevance: Proceedings of a Conference. Transactions of the Indian Institute of Advanced Study,* Volume Eleven (Simla: Indian Institute of Advanced Study, 1969), pp. 393-413; and (2) "Research Areas on Nonviolent Alternatives" in my *Exploring Nonviolent Alternatives,* pp. 73-113.

Numerous research problems and topics have been incorporated in this revision from suggestions made over the years by a large number of individuals in articles, memoranda, correspondence, and conversations. Acknowledgement is especially due to: Philip Bogdonoff, the late Hon. Alastair Buchan, April Carter, Theodor Ebert, Robert Irwin, Irving Janis, Jessie Jones, Daniel Katz, Herbert Kelman, Julia Kittross, Christopher Kruegler, Ronald McCarthy, Charles Nathan, Robert Nozick, the late Lars Porsholt, Adam Roberts, Theodor Roszak, Sandi Mandeville Tate, Kenneth Wadoski, and Kurt H. Wolff. Apologies to any who have unintentionally not been listed.

Several aides to thought, study, and action have been added to increase the usefulness of this booklet.

For editorial suggestions, I am grateful to David H. Albert, Philip Bogdonoff, Robert Irwin, and John McLeod. Philip Bogdonoff suggested the title.

Gene Sharp

Program on Nonviolent Sanctions in Conflict and Defense Center for International Affairs Harvard University Cambridge, Massachusetts June 1985

NATIONAL SECURITY THROUGH CIVILIAN-BASED DEFENSE

N ow, more than ever, we need to question some of our basic assumptions about defense, security, and peace, and to examine possible new policies that might help achieve those goals. The dangers and limitations of modern military means — conventional, nuclear, and chemical-biological — are too obvious to need repetition. What has not been clear is what alternative we have. This essay is focused on one alternative system of defense, which is called "civilian-based defense."[1] This policy may prove to be a superior way to provide national security — safety from attack — by dissuading and deterring potential attackers, and, if need be, waging effective defense against them.

The oft-posed choice between the acceptance of tyranny and the waging of war has been aggravated by developments in weapons technology, communications, and transportation. The technological changes in methods of war have brought about the concentration of large-scale military power in the hands of a few countries which possess scientific know-how, a technological and industrial base, and vast resources. In particular, the supremacy of the United States and the Soviet Union in capability for large-scale conventional and nuclear warfare has not yet been seriously challenged.

Dependency in defense

In consequence, most countries have found that in relation to the U.S. and U.S.S.R. their capacity for self-defense by conventional military means has been drastically reduced or destroyed altogether. This is true even for highly industrialized Western European countries, and the matter is more extreme for less developed countries.

At the same time, local conflicts have gained worldwide significance and led to direct involvement in one form or another by the superpowers. This gravitation of deterrence and defense tasks to the most powerful and most technologically developed countries has had a variety of undesirable results for the other countries.

For example, alliance with a superpower is not a guarantee of national security. The ultimate defense decision lies in foreign hands, and despite treaties a small power may be left helpless when threatened or attacked, as the fate of Czechoslovakia in 1939 illustrates. In 1968, Czechoslovakia was attacked by its own allies!

On the other hand, military help from a superpower can be highly dangerous for the people being "defended." Witness Vietnam. What would happen to West Berlin, or even West Germany, in case of powerful American military help to throw back a Russian invasion?

Dependence on stronger powers for defense may have other disadvantages. Do not the very people who want American military support frequently resent being dependent on it? Does not dependence on others for defense sometimes lead to reduced willingness to contribute to one's own defense? Does not such dependence often lead to an unwise stifling of one's own political judgment and autonomy in both domestic and foreign policies?

This shift of responsibility for the security of many nations to the superpowers has more than doubled the latter's defense tasks. Military commitments of the U.S. extend far beyond its own defense. Dozens of countries around the world depend on American support and pledges for their security. A similar situation exists on a smaller scale for the Soviet Union. Someday China may have a comparable status.

These foreign commitments (assuming good motives behind them) are for the United States an extraordinarily difficult and often thankless task. Even from a military perspective, there are severe problems involved in carrying out this world role.

Political problems are also severe. It is difficult to pose as a defender of freedom when that role seems to require alliances with dictatorships. Great sacrifices presented by government leaders as helping people prevent dictatorial rule are sometimes seen by others as unwanted efforts by the United States to be the world's policeman or, less flatteringly, as attempts to impose a new imperialism.

Some efforts to counter the gravitation of effective military capacity to the superpowers have begun. It has been proposed that Western Europe become a powerful independent military bastion. Some countries in conflicts with superpowers have shifted to guerrila warfare (Vietnam and Afghanistan) or nonviolent resistance (Czechoslovakia). This constitutes an asymmetrical conflict situation — in which the two sides fight by using different techniques.[2] A massive spread of military hardware to Third World countries has also occurred. All of these developments have their own problems, and do not fundamentally alter as yet the massive concentration of military capacity in the United States and the Soviet Union.

The Need for Self-defense

The local involvement of a superpower carries with it the additional danger of escalation into a larger international war. Other consequences include the drain of resources on the United States, the killing of Americans, the effects of such violence abroad on the society at home, and the distraction from other important domestic and international tasks.

This could all be changed if countries fearing military aggression or the imposition by violence of minority dictatorships had the capacity to defend themselves — in other words, if countries throughout the world were able, primarily by their own efforts, to defeat domestic or foreign-aided dictatorial groups of *any* political doctrine, as well as being able to deter and defeat international aggression against themselves.

The world security situation would then be very different, and would not "require" global American military involvement. There would be neither the need nor the excuse for worldwide military commitments of the United States or any other country. The superpowers could concentrate on their own defenses and devote their technical and financial superiority to constructive humanitarian ends.

Is this possible? How can the capacity for self-defense be restored if it has been destroyed by the very nature of modern military technology? We need to ask: Can there be a new concept of defense which is *not* dependent on military technology, but which could nevertheless be effective against real dangers? That could only happen if defense could be provided *without* military means — an idea inconceivable to most people.

Defense[3] has almost always meant military defense. This need no longer be true. The main question is: How can there be a nonmilitary defense?

We must start with basics. We have usually assumed that defense capacity and military power are identical, and that military occupation means political control. But these assumptions are not valid:

1. Military power today often exists without real capacity to *defend* in struggle the people and society relying upon it. Often it only threatens mutual annihiliation. More importantly — and this is the main argument of this essay — defense capacity can today be provided without military means.

2. Military occupation does *not* necessarily give the invader political control of the country, and the occupation can be destroyed *without* military resistance.

This is because all governments depend for the sources of their power on the cooperation and obedience of the population and the institutions of the society they would rule. That cooperation can be, and often has been, restricted or denied. This nonviolent non-cooperation, if maintained over time despite repression, will weaken and can destroy the government.[4] This prospect is especially likely when the regime is one of domestic usurpers or foreign invaders who have violated the society's standards of legitimacy.

It is sometimes argued that the traditional problem of defense against invasions has been outdated by nuclear weapons. That is not true. Invasions still occur and neither invasions themselves nor resistance to them need lead to use of nuclear weapons.

International aggression is usually launched to achieve certain objectives: territorial, political, economic, ideological, and the like. Massive radioactive annihilation of the attacked country prevents the achievement of such objectives. Therefore, while accidents and irrational destruction are always possible, the use of nuclear weapons is unlikely in international aggression unless they are launched (1) as a "preemptive strike" by a nuclear power itself fearing an imminent nuclear attack, or (2) as an escalation of weaponry in a conventional military conflict by one side to avoid defeat. Therefore, despite the existence of nuclear weapons, a nonmilitary defense policy is relevant and even essential for a country which wishes to avoid both foreign domination and nuclear destruction.

Direct Defense by Civilians

Civilian-based defense is such a policy. Its objectives are to deter and defeat foreign aggression and internal take-overs. This is done by prepared capacity of the civilian population to wage non-cooperation and defiance to deny the attackers their objectives and to make it impossible for them to establish and maintain political control over the country.

Civilian-based defense offers to the country adopting the policy the prospect of (1) providing effective deterrence and defense against invasions and internal take-overs; (2) avoiding escalation to nuclear weapons by resisting conventional attack with very different nonmilitary forms of struggle, and (3) removing completely the motives for a preemptive nuclear attack by the country being neither a possesor of nuclear weapons nor a base for their launching. We therefore need to give attention to the original defense problem of how to deter and defend against aggression.

People's motives for defending their society with this policy will for the most part be the same as their motives for defending by military means. They will likely love their country, way of life, and even the right of the citizens to disagree with each other on current issues and the future development of the society. They will likely cherish a heritage or newly achieved capacity to speak their minds, to believe as they choose, and to work together to preserve qualities from the past and to build a better society for the future. They need unite only on the simple point that no group of foreign invaders or internal usurpers is going to be permitted to rule and dominate them or to achieve their objectives by violent attack and repression. People will instead insist on their right to live without interference as they choose and to improve their society in the future as they may decide.

Military technology, through the introductions of the airplane, tank, and rocket, has in most cases long since abolished the possibility of effective geographical defense — that is protection of the territory and all within it by exclusion of the enemy forces and weapons. Indeed, battles over territory often directly contribute to massive deaths and physical destruction of the society being "defended." If we are to avoid that, we are thrown back to the people and their institutions applying a very different type of weapons for the direct defense of their freedoms and society, rather than battling over territory itself.

Instead of attempting by fighting over geographical points, people applying this policy actively defend their way of life, society, and freedoms directly. This is direct defense by the citizens themselves. The priorities of action are crucial. The maintenance of a free press, for example, or keeping the invader's propaganda out of the schools is of more direct importance to democracy than, say, possession of a given mountain or the killing of young conscripts in the invader's army. Large-scale preparations and training would be necessary to maximize the effectiveness of social, economic and political power against an invader or an internal take-over.

The citizens would prevent enemy control of the country by massive and selective refusal to cooperate and to obey, supporting instead the legal government and its call to resist. Police would refuse to locate and arrest patriotic opponents of the invader. Teachers would refuse to introduce the invader's propaganda into the schools — as happened in Norway under the Nazis. Workers and managers would use strikes, delays and obstructionism to impede exploitation of the country — as happened in the Ruhr in 1923. Clergymen would preach about the duty to refuse to help the invader — as happened in the Netherlands under the Nazis. Politicians, civil servants and judges, by ignoring or defying the enemy's illegal orders, would keep the normal machinery of government and the courts out of his control — as happened in the German resistance to the Kapp *Putsch* in 1920. Newspapers refusing to submit to censorship would be published illegally in large editions or many small editions — as happened in the Russian 1905 Revolution and in several Nazi-occupied countries. Free radio programs would continue from hidden transmitters — as happened in Czechoslovakia in August, 1968.[5]

In civilian-based defense struggles, the general citizenry and the society's institutions are themselves combatants. When successful, civilian-based defense of the society would lead to the collapse or withdrawal of the invader or internal usurper. The victory would follow from the successful direct defense of the society, not from battles over the control of geography.

Such defense is possible because a *coup d'etat* or invasion does not by a quick stroke achieve the attackers' objectives and give them control of the population and society. Even in the absence of resistance those take time and efforts. In face of well-prepared noncooperation and defiance major efforts will be required to attempt to gain those objectives and that control. Despite the attacker's efforts, both may be denied by a resistant civilian population determined to defend their society and skilled in doing so.

In addition, in case of invasion, civilian-based defense would set in motion restraining influences both in the invader's own country (stimulating dissension at home, splits in the regime, and, in extremes, even resistance) and in the international community (creating diplomatic pressures, political losses, and sometimes economic sanctions) that would be inimical to the invader's interests and to his attempts at consolidating an occupation.

This may sound unlikely, but there is more evidence now that civilian-based defense can work than there was in 1939 for the practicability of nuclear weapons, intercontinental rockets, and trips to the moon.

Nevertheless, the idea that national defense may be exercised more effectively by the vigilance and trained nonviolent resistance of citizens than by military means seems startling to some and ridiculous to others. There is no denying that there would be risks and dangers involved in such a policy. These need, however, to be measured against the risks and dangers of the military deterrence policies currently in operation.

The Need for Critical Examination

Contrary to present assumptions, there is a long history of non-violent political struggle. Despite lack of knowledge of its requirements, and in the absence of training and preparations, this technique has produced some impressive results, even against high odds.

There are as yet no cases in which prepared civilian-based defense has caused an invader to withdraw — because there has never yet been a case of prepared civilian-based defense being used as a country's official defense policy. (There are, of course, cases of effective unprepared resistance in occupied countries.) The formulation of a civilian-based defense policy is a deliberate attempt to advance beyond where we are now, an attempt based upon a serious calculation of political realities and possibilities.

Given the resources and the commitment, there is reason to believe progress can be made in devising political strategies of nonviolent action calculated to control tyrants and preserve political freedom. With political research and analysis, we could locate and come to understand the weaknesses of occupation regimes and of totalitarian systems. We could then concentrate resistance against them on their weak points, using what might be called a form of "political *karate.*"

Even *without* advance preparations, the people of Czechoslovakia provided an experiment in the use of nonviolent struggle in their response to the Russian invasion and occupation. The Dubček regime held out from August until April, while the Russians expected to be able to overcome possible Czech military resistance within days. We need to learn from the strengths and weaknesses of this case.

Civilian-based defense ought to be subjected to an examination and consideration at least as rigorous as that devoted to any proposal for a major change in defense policy. Concrete examination has to be given to the many practical problems involved in waging civilian-based defense, to possible strategies, to types of repression that would need to be anticipated, and to the question of the casualties. The argument, therefore, is not for the adoption of civilian-based defense now, but for research, investigation and official consideration. The aim is not to win converts, but to provoke thought.

Begin With the Known

As a first step, civilian-based defense must draw upon the known experience of nonviolent struggle, without being limited by it, in order to develop viable strategies to deter and defeat attacks on a country.

The study of cases of nonviolent action[6] has been largely neglected by strategists, historians and social scientists. Serious research to correct this neglect has only begun. Moreover, the situation has been aggravated by a series of misunderstandings about the nature of nonviolent action which need to be corrected.

Nonviolent action, the major instrument of a civilian-based defense policy, is the opposite of passivity and cowardice. It is not simply persuasion, but the wielding of power. It does not assume that humans are inherently "good." It has been mostly used by "ordinary" people. It does not absolutely require shared principles or a high degree of common interest between the contending groups. It may work by "nonviolent coercion." *At least* as "Western" as it is "Eastern," the technique is designed for struggle against a repressive, violent opponent. It may be used to defend as well as to change a government, and has been widely applied against foreign occupations and even against totalitarian systems.

There are many instances of effective nonviolent action, including: the early resistance by American colonists, 1763-1775; Hungarian passive resistance vs. Austrian rule, especially 1850-1867; Finland's disobedience and political noncooperation against Russia, 1898-1905; the Russian 1905 Revolution, and that of February, 1917 (before the October Bolshevik *coup*); the Korean nonviolent protest against Japanese rule, 1919-1922 (which failed); the Indian 1930-1931 independence campaign; German government-sponsored resistance to the Franco-Belgian occupation of the Ruhr in 1923.

Later examples include: resistance in several Nazi-occupied countries, especially Norway, the Netherlands and Denmark; governmental and popular measures to nullify anti-Jewish measures in several Nazi-allied and Nazi-occupied countries, such as Bulgaria, Italy, France and Denmark; the toppling by popular noncooperation and defiance of the dictators of El Salvador and Guatemala in 1944; the 1963 and 1966 campaigns of the Buddhists against the governments of South Vietnam.

Other recent cases involve resistance, uprisings and less dramatic pressures for liberalization in communist-ruled countries, including the 1953 East German uprising, strikes in the Soviet political prisoner camps in 1953, major aspects of the 1956 Hungarian revolution, Polish popular pressures for reforms, efforts for de-Stalinization in the Soviet Union, popular pressures for liberalization in Czechoslovakia early in 1968 and popular and governmental noncooperation following the Russian invasion in August. Poland, during the struggles of Solidarity both for democratization and against martial law is an important case.

Nonviolent resistance has occurred against totalitarian systems, on an improvised basis and despite the absence of training, preparations and know-how. It should be noted that totalitarians like Hitler deliberately sought to promote the impression of their regime's omnipotence, both domestically and internationally, to discourage any potential opposition.

Totalitarian and other dictatorial systems contain critical weaknesses in the form of inefficiencies, internal conflicts, and factors contributing to impermanence. It is precisely these features that offer themselves up for exploitation by civilian-based defense strategies.[7] However, the basic reason why this policy can be effective against totalitarian systems is that even such extreme political systems cannot free themselves entirely from dependence on their subjects. As an articulated strategy, civilian-based defense is designed to deny totalitarian rulers the compliance, cooperation and submission they require.

One hundred ninety-eight specific methods of nonviolent action have been identified. These methods are classified under three broad categories: protest and persuasion, noncooperation, and intervention.[8] Methods of nonviolent protest and persuasion are largely symbolic demonstrations, including parades, marches and vigils (54 methods). Noncooperation is divided into three sub-categories: a) social noncooperation (16 methods), b) economic noncooperation, including boycotts (26 methods) and strikes (23 methods), and c) acts of political noncooperation (38 methods). "Nonviolent intervention," by psychological, physical, social, economic, or political means, includes 41 methods (such as the fast, nonviolent occupation, and parallel government).

The use of a considerable number of these methods — carefully chosen, on a large scale, persistently, with wise strategy and tactics, by trained civilians — is likely to cause any illegitimate regime severe problems.

Nonviolent action resembles military war more than it does negotiation; it is a technique of struggle. As such, nonviolent action involves the use of power, but in different ways than military violence. Instead of confronting the opponent's apparatus of violence with comparable forces, the nonviolent actionists counter with political weapons. The degree to which noncooperation will threaten the opponent's power position varies, but its potential is best illustrated in the disruptive effects of massive strikes and in mutinies of the opponent's troops.

The violent antagonist's repressive measures — arrests, imprisonment, beatings, concentration camps, shootings, executions and other means — are hardly insignificant, but *in themselves* are not decisive. In fact, the opponent's repression is evidence of the power of nonviolent action, and is no more reason for despair than if, in a regular war, the enemy shoots back.[9]

If the civilian defenders maintain their discipline and persist despite repression, and if they involve significant sections of the populace in the struggle, the opponent's will can be retarded and finally blocked. If leaders are arrested, the movement may carry on without a recognizable leadership. The opponent may declare new acts illegal, only to find that he has opened up new opportunities for defiance.

There is a strong tendency for the opponent's violence and repression to react against his power position. This is called "political *jiu-jitsu.*" Against disciplined and persistent nonviolent actionists, the opponent's violence can never really come to grips with the kind of power they wield. Under certain conditions repression may make more people join the resistance. The opponent's supporters may become uneasy, disobey, and even defect. The numbers of civilian defenders may become so large that control becomes impossible. The opponent's police may give up, officials occasionally resign, and sometimes troops may even mutiny. Massive nonviolent defiance by the population has by then made the enemy government powerless. Defeat of the nonviolent actionists is always possible, just as defeat occurs in traditional war. Victory with this technique will come only to those who have developed it into a refined and powerful political tool.

Transarmament

Civilian-based defense[10] depends primarily on a trained civilian population to defend the country's freedom and independence by social, psychological, economic and political means. The population could be prepared through regular democratic processes and government decisions. Long before the change-over from military defense to civilian-based defense — a process called *transarmament* — considerable research, investigation, and analysis would be needed. Highly important, too, would be widespread public study, thinking, discussion and debate on the nature, feasibility, merits, and problems of civilian-based defense and all of the forms its exercise might take.

After the decision to transarm, a Department of Civilian-based Defense might be set up to provide planning, analysis, coordination and some leadership. All this would probably be more complex than planning for military defense.

No country is going to abandon military defense without confidence in a substitute defense policy.[11] Therefore, for a significant period, civilian-based defense preparations would be carried out alongside military measures, until the latter could be phased out as no longer needed. During the transarmament period, personnel and money would be needed for both.

A major educational program for the whole country on the nature and purpose of civilian-based defense would be required. Federal, state and local governmental bodies, assisted by independent institutions such as schools, churches, trade unions, business groups, newspapers, television and the like could undertake this. People would be informed about the broad outlines of the new policy, the ways it would operate, and the results expected. This would help them decide if they want such a policy.

Certain occupational groups, including those wishing to participate in advanced aspects of the policy, would need specialized training. Such training would vary in its character and purpose, ranging from that required by local neighborhood defense workers to specialist education at academies and colleges. This is not to say that there is no role for spontaneity within the scope of civilian-based defense, but that it is a limited role. Even then, it needs to be self-disciplined and rooted in thorough understanding of the requirements of nonviolent action and the chosen civilian-based defense strategies.

In crises, specialists in civilian-based defense might play an important role in initiating resistance, especially at the beginning of an occupation or a *coup*. In various situations they could serve as special cadres for particularly dangerous tasks. Some specialists might be kept in reserve to guide the later stages of the resistance. However, they could not — and should not be expected to — carry out the resistance *for* the general population. Responsibility for the main thrust of civilian-based defense must be assumed by the citizenry. Since the leaders generally would be among the first imprisoned or otherwise incapacitated by the usurper, the population must be able to continue on its own initiative.

Maximizing Impact

Preparations for civilian-based defense would not consist simply of instructions arrived at by a centralized leadership and carried out at the lower levels. An effective strategy would require an analysis of the potentialities of many factors — means of transportation, government departments, schools, and so forth — to identify the specific points at which noncooperation might have a maximum impact in preventing any illegal group from seizing control. Ordinary people in jobs at those places would often be the best sources of the intelligence information needed to make these decisions. To make accurate tactical judgements, however, one would need knowledge of the forms and strategies of nonviolent resistance, the enemy's weaknesses, the kinds of repression to expect, the crucial political issues on which to resist, and many practical questions of how to implement the resistance.

The setting up of an underground system of contacts would probably have to wait until a crisis, to make it harder for the opponent to know the exact personnel and structure of the resistance organization. However, "war games" and civilian-based defense maneuvers could offer the specialists a chance to examine the viability of alternative strategies and tactics for dealing with various types of threats. Training maneuvers in which imaginary occupations or takeovers would be met by civilian resistance could be acted out at levels ranging from local residential areas, offices or factories to cities, states and even the whole country.

Technical preparations would also be necessary for civilian-based defense. Provisions and equipment would be required for communications with the population after the enemy had occupied key centers and seized established newspapers, radio stations and other mass media. Equipment to publish underground newspapers and resistance leaflets and to make broadcasts could be hidden beforehand. It might be possible to make advance arrangements for locating such broadcasting stations or printing plants in the territory of a friendly neighboring country as part of a civilian-based defense mutual aid agreement.

Since an enemy might seek to force the population into submission by starvation, and since certain resistance methods (e.g., a general strike) would disrupt distribution of food, emergency supplies of staples should be stored locally. Alternative means of providing fuel and water during emergencies could also be explored. For certain types of crises, plans might be considered for the dispersal of large groups of people from big cities to rural areas where the oppressor would find it more difficult to exercise control over them.

Because civilian-based defense requires the active support and participation of the populace (*not* necessarily unanimity, however), the citizens must have both the *will* and *ability* to defend their society in crises. For citizens to have the will to defend their democratic system does not imply that they believe the system is perfect. It does mean that the system is preferable to any regime likely to be imposed by internal take-over or by foreign invaders, and that any necessary changes in the system should be made by democratic decision. For effective civilian-based defense, people have to *want* to resist threats to their freedom and independence. They must genuinely cherish the democratic qualities of their society.

Measures to increase the effectiveness of civilian-based defense (including the decentralization of control in order to make citizens more self-reliant in facing emergencies) are likely to contribute to the vitality of democratic society, and to increased participation in it. With civilian-based defense, therefore, there is no rivalry or contradiction between defense requirements and domestic needs; they are complementary. In the case of the U.S., this would be a considerable advance over present military policy, which has delivered us into exactly that contradiction.

Civilian-based defense is thus a democractic defense of democracy. Just as tyranny and war, in their cyclical appearances, may be mutually-reinforcing causes, so political freedom and peace may be intimately connected.[12] A civilian-based defense policy may provide concrete means for producing a condition of life that allows for the interplay and perpetual renewal of the last two qualities in place of the first two.

Aggressor's Considerations

An aggressive regime deciding whether or not to invade another country will usually consider: 1) the expected ease or difficulty of the invasion and subsequent control of the country, and 2) the anticipated gains as compared to costs (human, economic, political, ideological, prestigial, military and other). Except in the case of a nation acting on a huge gamble or pure irrationality, the likelihood of considerably greater losses than gains will probably deter the invader.

Invasion is not an objective in and of itself. It is a way to achieve a wider purpose, which almost always involves occupation of the invaded country. If, however, a successful invasion is followed by immense difficulties in occupying and controlling the country, its society and population, the invasion's "success" becomes for its perpetrators a dangerous mirage. Certainly the Russians invading Czechoslovakia encountered at the early stages great and unanticipated difficulties. Advance civilian-based defense preparations and training could have considerably increased these. Where preparations and training are thorough, a would-be invader might perceive that he will not be able to rule successfully the country that he might easily invade. Civilian-based defense has at that moment revealed itself as a powerful deterrent.

There are other contingencies a would-be aggressor would need to think through. A population's spirit and methods of resistance could well spread to other countries and again be applied against the aggressor's tyranny elsewhere. In such a light, civilian-based defense has to be considered as a possible nonnuclear deterrent to conventional attack.

Could civilian-based defense deter a nuclear attack? No, not in the strict sense of "deter." However, this policy could by other influences dissuade a potential attacker and drastically reduce the chances of a nuclear attack. It is sometimes argued that civilian-based defense is nonsense in the nuclear age, since it would provide no defense should nuclear bombs and rockets start falling. The present system, however, cannot *defend* against that contingency either. The question, rather, is whether the conditions likely to be produced by transarmament to civilian-based defense will encourage or discourage the launching of a nuclear attack on a country which has transarmed to this policy.

Deterrence and Defense

Who fears and expects a nuclear attack the most today, and who the least? It is precisely the nuclear powers who most fear nuclear attack, partly because each side is afraid of the other. Mexico, Canada and Australia — all *without* nuclear weapons — fear and expect nuclear attack far less than the U.S. and U.S.S.R.

Fear of nuclear attack, then, or fear of military defeat in a major conventional war, may be a strong reason for launching a nuclear attack on the enemy. Civilian-based defense, which can only be used for *defensive* purposes, would remove that motive, and hence, if not cancel out the danger, at least greatly reduce it. It is certainly significant that several military men to whom this problem has been presented do not see much likelihood of a nuclear attack against a country employing only civilian-based defense as a deterrent.

No deterrent can ever be *guaranteed* to deter. The failure of the nuclear deterrent could permanently end all talk of alternative deterrents as well as the talkers and nontalkers. But the failure of the civilian-based defense deterrent would still permit human life to continue and long-range hope for a just solution to remain, while the struggle against tyranny would enter a new stage with a more direct confrontation of forces. When the deterrence capacity of civilian-based defense fails, a series of contingency plans to deal with the new situation comes into operation with the potential to win a real political and human victory.

Although resistance is never easy, it is less difficult to resist a tyrannical regime while it is seeking to establish itself than after it has succeeded. George Kennan pointed out that for a successful seizure of power by a totalitarian regime "a certain degree of mass bewilderment and passivity are required." Advance preparations and training for civilian-based defense are designed specifically to prevent that condition. The invader will encounter a population well prepared to fight for its freedom with methods which, precisely because they are nonviolent, will be especially insidious and dangerous to the occupation regime. In the end, the attacker may well lose.

Of course, civilian-based defense cannot keep enemy troops from entering the country. The enemy's entry is an illusion of easy success; it operates as a political ambush. The people will not have allowed themselves to succumb to the psychological condition that Hitler prescribed for successful occupation; they will not have admitted defeat and recognized the occupation regime as their conqueror and master.

Under civilian-based defense, the country and the defense capacity would not have been defeated. The combat strength would not yet have been applied. The citizenry, trained and prepared, would not feel dismayed or confused. They would understand that the distribution of enemy soldiers and functionaries throughout the country did not mean defeat but instead was the initial stage of a longer struggle at close range. This would be difficult, but the civilian defenders would hold advantages. Set-backs might occur; these could lead, however, to rebuilding strength for future campaigns. There are no white flags of surrender in civilian-based defense.

Although civilian-based defense cannot defend the geographic borders — military means cannot do so either — some limited action would be taken even at the initial stage. The deployment of troops could be delayed by obstructionist activities at the docks (if troops came by sea), by refusal to operate the railroads, or by blocking highways and airports with thousands of abandoned automobiles.

Such acts would make clear to the individual enemy soldiers that, whatever they might have been told, they were not welcome as an invasion force. As other symbolic actions the people could wear mourning bands, stay at home, stage a limited general strike, defy curfews, or urge the invading soldiers not to believe their government's propaganda. Such actions would give notice to friend and foe that the occupation will be firmly resisted and at the same time build up the people's morale so as to prevent submission and collaboration.

The invader's parades of troops through the cities would be met by conspicuously empty streets and shuttered windows, and any public receptions would be boycotted. Efforts would be made to undermine the loyalty of his individual soldiers and functionaries. They would be informed that there will be resistance, but that the resistance will be of a special type, directed against the attempt to seize control but without threatening harm to them as individuals. If this could be communicated, the soldiers might be more likely to help the resisting population in small ways, to avoid brutalities, and to mutiny at a crisis point, than they would if they expected at any moment to be killed by snipers or plastic bombs.

Forms of Noncooperation

There would be early forms of more substantial political and economic noncooperation. For example, the invader might meet a blanket refusal by the government bureaucracy and civil servants to carry out his instructions. Or, these officials might continue the old policies, ignore his orders, and disrupt the implementation of new policies. The police might refuse to make political arrests for the invader, warn people of impending arrests, selectively refuse certain orders or carry them out inefficiently.

Attempts to exploit the economic system might be met with limited general strikes, slow-downs, refusal of assistance by or disappearance of indispensable experts, and the selective use of various types of strikes at key points in industries, transportation and the supply of raw materials. News of resistance might be publicized through prearranged channels throughout the world, and also be beamed at the invader's homeland. These are only illustrations. Since each case is different, and the enemy's objectives are crucial, obviously there can be no one blueprint for all situations. And it would be important to plan different possible types of strategies for dealing with diverse threats.

Over the long run, both injuries and deaths are to be expected, though they are likely to be much fewer than in military struggles. If the citizens are unwilling to face the prospect of such casualties in their defense, resistance will surely collapse; similarly, in a conventional war defeat is certain if the troops run the other way or surrender when fired upon. In this, as in any struggle, casualties must be seen in the context of the campaign as a whole. It is remarkable how many people who accept as natural millions of dead and wounded in a military war find the dangers of execution and suffering in civilian-based defense a decisive disadvantage; to the contrary, there is evidence that casualty rates in nonviolent struggles are much smaller than in regular warfare.

Success and Failure

As the occupation develops, the enemy may try to gain control of various institutions, such as the courts, schools, unions, cultural groups, professional societies and the like. If that control is achieved, the future capacity for resistance will be weakened for a long period. Therefore, civilian-based defense must firmly resist any efforts of the invader to control the society's institutions. A few examples will show how this could be done.

The courts would declare the invader's bureaucracy an illegal and unconstitutional body; they would continue to operate on the basis of pre-invasion laws and constitutions, and they would refuse to give moral support to the invader, even if they had to close the courts and maintain order by social pressures, solidarity, and non-violent sanctions. Attempts to control the school curriculum would be met with refusal to change the school curriculum or to introduce the invader's propaganda, explanations to the pupils of the issues at stake, continuation of regular education as long as possible, and, if necessary, closing the schools and holding private classes in the children's homes.

Efforts to dominate trade unions or professional groups could be met by persistence in abiding by their preinvasion constitutions and procedures, denial of recognition to new organizations set up by or for the invader, refusal to pay dues or attend meetings of any new pro-invader organizations, and the carrying out of disruptive strikes and economic and political boycotts.

In considering the possibility of failure of civilian-based defense, or of only very limited success, two factors need to be kept in mind. First, even failure after an heroic struggle by civilian-based defense would be preferable to any outcome of a major nuclear war. At worst, it would mean a long, difficult and painful existence under severe tyranny, but life would go on, and with life the hope for eventual freedom. Nonviolent action is not a course for cowards. It requires the ability and determination to sustain the battle whatever the price in suffering, yet it would, in the most disastrous case imaginable, still allow a future for humankind. And second, in this kind of struggle, failure to achieve total victory would not mean total defeat. Even if the population were unable to drive out the invader, it could maintain a considerable degree of autonomy for the country, and for its institutions upon whose independence any country's freedom largely depends.

The other side of the argument for civilian-based defense is that under present international and technological conditions this system offers a greater chance of real success in opposing occupation or regaining political freedom than does military defense. When the usurper fails to bring the occupied country to heel, a miasma of uncertainty and dissent could grow within his regime and among his soldiers and officials. International pressures could further weaken the oppressor and strengthen the civilian defenders. Very likely, the usurper would find that he faced not only the opposition of world opinion but also significant diplomatic moves and economic embargoes. Continued repression in the occupied country could feed further resistance. The multiplication of non-cooperating and disobedient subjects would be aimed to defeat the would-be tyrant and bring about a restoration of liberty, enhanced with new meaning, vitality and durability.

The exact way that victory would come would vary from one situation to another. In one case it might coincide with a change of government in the invading country. Or there might be negotiations, with some face-saving formula for the invader. In extremes, the occupation force itself might be so near disintegration and mutiny that with or without such a formula the troops and functionaries would simply go home. In any case, the real meaning would be clear: the occupation would have been defeated.

Another way of looking at civilian-based defense is to realize that it is *not* disarmament, if disarmament means the reduction or abandonment of defense capacity. Instead, the change-over to civilian defense is *transarmament* — the substitution of a new defense capacity that provides deterrence and defense without conventional and nuclear military power. It also contributes to world peace, since unlike military means civilian-based defense cannot be used for, or misperceived as intended for, international aggression.

A Policy, Not a Creed

Nor is civilian-based defense a new doctrine for which unquestioning "believers" are sought. It is a defense policy, not a creed. The development of civilian-based defense, in theory and practice, is still in its early stages. Those who have examined the idea differ in their judgements of the types of defense problems, and of enemies, for which it might be suitable. For example, some say it is not possible against a Nazi-type regime, but that it would work against occupation regimes of medium severity. There is also anything but uniformity of opinion about military defense policies!

Another crucial point about civilian-based defense is that it is possible for only one or a few countries to adopt the policy initially, without treaties and while most countries remain militarily armed. When convinced of its effectiveness and advantages, other countries too may transarm. Aggressive regimes may well have to be taught lessons concerning the resistance capacity of civilian-based defense countries.

The first nations to adopt civilian-based defense are likely to be those that most want self-reliance in defense but which lack the ability to do this with their own military means. The super-powers may well follow far behind. It does not, of course, have to be that way, and surprises may occur. A considerable period would doubtless exist in which some countries had transarmed to civilian-based defense while many others retained military defense — and some of the latter might never change over.

There would inevitably be strongholds of resistance to adoption of this policy. Democratic countries with large military establishments are unlikely, and probably unable, to eliminate these in a short span of time. They might, however, add a civilian-based defense component, if its effectiveness could be convincingly demonstrated. They might increasingly rely on this component, gradually phasing out the military sector, until the substitution was completed. Some military personnel could no doubt be retrained to fit into the new civilian-based defense system.

Dictatorial regimes and unstable governments probably would cling hardest to military capacity for both domestic and international purposes. However, even dictatorships could be influenced toward civilian-based defense, both by removal of fear of foreign military attack (contributing to internal political relaxation) and by nonviolent pressures for change from their own populations.

It is impossible to predict with certainty the international consequences of the initial cases of transarmament. A nation's decision to adopt a policy of civilian-based defense and its effectiveness in carrying it out will depend on the state of knowledge of this kind of struggle, the adequacy of the strategic planning, preparations, and training, geographical location, the nature of its enemies, and the determination, skill, and heroism of the people.

Domestic and International Consequences

The successful defeat of a seizure of power or an occupation by a systematic civilian-based defense policy might make a significant contribution toward the adoption of such a policy by other countries. Initial successes of this policy are likely to lead more and more countries to investigate it and finally to transarm.

Countries that had already adopted civilian-based defense could directly encourage other nations to transarm. Under "Civilian-based Defense Mutual Assistance Pacts" several countries could share knowledge, research results, and experience. They could provide certain aid in emergencies (such as food, supplies, finances, diplomatic and economic pressures, a haven for refugees, safe printing and broadcasting facilities). They could give technical advice to countries considering civilian-based defense, and undertake joint activities to deter aggression by this means.

In contrast with military planning, a sharing of results of civilian-based defense research, planning and training would not endanger future combat effectiveness. It would instead accelerate the rate at which countries transarmed to civilian-based defense. This would be of major importance in a step-by-step removal of war from the international scene, and in increasing world security. It is important to note also that even if some countries never abandon military capacity, this would not be a reason for abandoning civilian-based defense, but rather for expanding it and improving its effectiveness.

Some of the important consequences of civilian-based defense will be social and economic. For example, transarmament to civilian-based defense by poor developing countries would probably mean that a large percentage of their present inordinate military budgets could be spent on dealing with poverty and development. Likewise, the developed countries would be able to give more help to the developing world after they convert to civilian-based defense.

Civilian-based defense can also deal with domestic or foreign-aided *coups d'etat* against the legal government, for which military defense is not designed. (Furthermore, it is usually the military establishment which overthrows the legal government, as in Greece in 1967.)

In the long run, civilian-based defense would be significantly cheaper than military defense, although it would not be inexpensive. The transition period, with both military and civilian-based defense preparations, might be quite expensive.

Another side benefit of civilian-based defense is that it is likely to make the means of defense serve democratic political ends positively, rather than requiring a foreign policy and alliances that violate a country's avowed democratic principles. No longer would it be necessary in the name of "defense" to make military alliances with dictatorships or to give tacit support to oppressive governments in order to keep military bases. In short, civilian-based defense would very likely become a potent force around the world for liberalizing or overthrowing tyrannical regimes.

But most importantly, civilian-based defense could be expected to restore a very high degree of self-reliance in defense to all countries. It would do this by shifting the source of defense power from modern technology to people themselves, to their determination and ability to act. If the nations of the world were able, predominantly by their own efforts, and above all without military assistance from the super powers, to defend themselves from internal usurpation by violent minorities and from foreign invasions, the security problems of the world would be altered fundamentally.

The Large Assumption

All of this discussion, of course, is based upon a large assumption: that today's elementary idea of civilian-based defense can be refined and developed to produce a new kind of defense policy at least as effective as military means. A considerable period of time given over to specific problem-oriented research will be needed to develop the general principles and theoretical frameworks of this policy, to produce models that may lend themselves to adaptation to a particular country's needs, and to complete planning, preparations, training, and other difficult tasks for the transarmament period.

Certainly all would agree that no reasonable possible solution to the problems of modern war and tyranny, and of effective defense against aggression and internal takeovers should be left uninvestigated. It is important now to start the exploration, thought, discussion and research that are needed to make possible a fair evaluation of this concept, and, if it turns out to be workable, to provide the basic knowledge necessary for transarmament, which could be completed within our lifetimes. We are now at a stage in the development of civilian-based defense at which major advances could be achieved relatively quickly.

Increased confidence in civilian-based defense and liberation by nonviolent action could produce a chain reaction in the progressive abolition of both war and tyranny. If this happened, the whole course of history would be altered. Some of the gravest fears and insecurities of the modern world would be lifted. Civilian-based defense could make it possible to face the future realistically, without fear or panic, but with courage, confidence and hope.

Notes

1. For a definition of civilian-based defense, see "Key Definitions" following this essay.

2. On asymmetrical conflicts, see Gene Sharp, *The Politics of Nonviolent Action* (Boston: Porter Sargent Publisher, 1973), pp. 451-454.

3. For a definition of defense, see "Key Definitions."

4. On this power theory, see Sharp, *The Politics of Nonviolent Action*, Chapter One, "The Nature and Control of Political Power," pp. 7-62, and Sharp, *Social Power and Political Freedom* (Boston: Porter Sargent Publishers, 1980), Chapter Two, "Social Power and Political Freedom," pp. 21-67.

5. For more details of these cases and references to them see indexed citations in Sharp, *The Politics of Nonviolent Action*, passim, and Adam Roberts, editor, *Civilian Resistance as a National Defense* (Harrisburg: Stackpole Books, 1968), British title: *The Strategy of Civilian Defence* (London: Faber & Faber, 1957), *passim*.

6. For a definition of nonviolent action, see "Key Definitions." For a discussion of its characteristics, see Sharp, *The Politics of Nonviolent Action,* Chapter Two, "Nonviolent Action: An Active Technique of Struggle," pp. 63-105.

7. On the weaknesses of dictatorial systems, see Gene Sharp, *Social Power and Political Freedom,* "Facing Dictatorships With Confidence," pp. 91-112.

8. On these methods, see Sharp, *The Politics of Nonviolent Action,* Part Two, "The Methods of Nonviolent Action," pp. 107-445.

9. On the dynamics and mechanisms of nonviolent struggle in face of a violent opponent, see Sharp, *The Politics of Nonviolent Action,* Part Three, "The Dynamics of Nonviolent Action," pp. 447-817.

10. For other, often fuller, discussions of civilian-based defense and transarmament, see the entries on the policy in the "For Further Reading" section following this essay.

11. For an analysis of why a substitute defense policy is required, see Sharp, *Social Power and Political Freedom,* Chapter Ten, "Seeking a Solution to the Problem of War," pp. 263-284.

12. On these interrelationships, see Sharp, *Social Power and Political Freedom,* Chapter Eleven, "The Societal Imperative," pp. 285-308, and Chapter Twelve, "Popular Empowerment," pp. 325-356.

TEN POINTS ABOUT
CIVILIAN-BASED DEFENSE

1. There is a need for effective national defense (strictly defined) against attack, and for "attack prevention" measures, including "deterrence" in its broadest sense.

2. The past approaches to "peace" and the abolition of war by both governments and private groups have largely failed, or have been of very limited utility.

3. There exists an undeveloped and unrefined nonviolent technique of struggle, which takes political, social, psychological, and economic forms. This technique has a vast history and has demonstrated a significant degree of effectiveness, despite past improvisation and lack of preparations, even against extreme regimes.

4. This technique has been used in a few cases for national defense purposes spontaneously or by official decision but always without research, preparations, or training (most significantly in Czechoslovakia, 1968-69; also in the Ruhr, Germany 1923; vs. the Kapp *Putsch,* Germany, 1920; Korea, 1919-1922; Nazi-occupied countries, 1939-1945; Poland against martial law, 1981-1982; etc.).

5. Proposals exist for deliberate development of the nonviolent technique of struggle by research, analysis, planning, and training. This could then become the basis of a new defense

policy which would use for defense a refined technique of nonviolent struggle. This would be waged by a trained civilian population on the basis of advance preparations and contingency plans against foreign conventional military attacks and internal usurpations. This substitute policy would aim to make the populace unrulable by the attackers and to deny the latter their objectives.

6. If viable and accurately perceived, this potentially could deter the initial attack, or cause the attempted occupation or internal usurpation to collapse, possibly quickly.

7. If so, and if the nuclear question could be satisfactorily resolved, a viable substitute for defensive war and civil war to defend the legitimate government and independence of the society would exist.

8. A phased program of "transarmament" could then be worked out for the gradual build-up of the "civilian-based defense" component and the eventual phasing down and out of the military defense component, by single countries or groups of countries. (Some countries might choose to keep both capacities.)

9. Civilian-based defense could break the technological weaponry spiral, restore self-defense capacity to small and medium-sized countries, and bypass major problems of negotiated disarmament and control treaties and agreements. These factors may have significant impacts in reducing the nuclear danger.

10. Major basic research, analysis, and feasibility studies for specific countries and areas are needed, in the form of a crash ten-year program with the support of very significant resources. This would be expected to provide evidence, insights, and contingency plans on which to base an informed evaluation of the potential merits of this policy.

QUESTIONS ABOUT THE APPLICABILITY OF CIVILIAN-BASED DEFENSE

1. Can people and societies give up military capacities without a substitute deterrence and defense policy? Why or why not? How?

2. What types of preparations and training may increase the capacity of populations to struggle by nonviolent means and enhance their chances of success?

3. Is civilian-based defense obviously of more interest to certain types of countries than to others?

4. What particular possible uses of civilian-based defense appear to be most realistic or possible?
   —by single countries to deter and defeat coups d'état?
   —by single countries to deter and defeat foreign invasions?
   —by single countries as an additional, or back-up, option within a predominantly military policy?
   —by members of an alliance as an additional option against coups and/or invasions?
   —as a key component in a phased multi-country or regional demilitarization plan (as in Central Europe, Northern Europe, etc.)?

5. What, if any, are the possible relationships of civilian-based defense to the problems of nuclear arms control and nuclear proliferation?

6. Could civilian-based defense be relevant to meeting the perceived

defense needs of Western European countries at present and in the coming decades?

7. Could civilian-based defense be relevant to meeting Japan's perceived defense needs?

8. What may be the utility and potential of plans for noncooperation in case of a presidential usurpation in the United States?

9. If one assumes that the superpowers are likely to be among the last to transarm fully to civilian-based defense, what interim steps could the United States take in that direction? How might it react to, aid, or oppose gradual transarmament of its European allies?

10. What might be the relevance of civilian-based defense to the needs of third world countries? To societies which have recently thrown off an established dictatorship?

11. What could be the roles of United Nations bodies and agencies in:
—investigation and development of civilian-based defense?
—assisting steps in transarmament for individual countries or groups of countries?
—providing supplementary assistance to countries which have transarmed and are waging civilian-based defense against a coup or international aggression?
—providing technical assistance, the results of research, policy studies, preparation and training planning, transarmament steps, and the like to countries which are considering or adopting the policy?

12. What might be the roles of single countries, alliances, national private bodies, and nongovernmental international organizations in providing to countries which are considering or adopting the policy those same types of technical assistance?

13. What could be the roles of regional and continental intergovernmental organizations in the investigation, transarmament, and waging of civilian-based defense?

14. What is the potential of Civilian-based Defense Mutual Aid Pacts among transarmed and transarming countries?

15. What may be the international consequences of transarmament:

—reduction of tensions?
—increased international aggression?
—aggravation of fears felt by dictatorial regimes?
—in economics?
—a spread of transarming countries?
—in long-term consequences for the international system?

16. What may be the consequences of transarmament within given countries:
—political?
—economic?
—social and psychological?
—for foreign policy and international participation?

17. How can basic research, problem-solving research, and policy studies on the nature and problems of civilian-based defense be best initiated, financed, and conducted?

18. What ought and can be done to disseminate information about the policy for examination by the public, policy specialists, national defense and international security analysts, defense departments and international bodies?

STEPS IN CONSIDERATION OF CIVILIAN-BASED DEFENSE

T hose individuals and groups which conclude that this alternative defense policy merits wider attention and consideration may take any of a variety of steps to achieve that end.

The aim of these activities — this is very important — is to extend knowledge, stimulate thought, and encourage a continuing evaluation of this policy on the basis of how adequately or otherwise it is able to meet the perceived defense and security threats of particular countries and parts of the world. As this is a policy, not a doctrine or set of beliefs, the aim is not to gain converts and "believers." It also must not be tied to some philosophy, creed, or proposed political panacea.

This policy needs to be presented relevant to a variety of political viewpoints and perspectives, depending on developing assessments of its capacity — in comparison with military policies — to deter and defend against various dangers.

Recognition of the reality of a variety of past, present, and possible future dangers of national and international origins is important as a starting point. Presentations which naively deny such dangers, or which attribute innocence where it doubtfully exists, will be understandably dismissed by many concerned people.

Civilian-based defense is still in its youthful, immature, stage of development. Its analysts are still identifying likely problems in its application. An attitude of exploration, recognition of its many problems, and advocacy of efforts to seek solutions to those problems is therefore necessary. Those problems need, in due course, to be compared to the often neglected problems of the practice of military deterrence and defense policies. This attitude of searching for possible solutions to difficult problems will bring respect and encourage thought by others about new possibilities.

Efforts to bring wider attention and consideration to civilian-based defense need to be focused exclusively on the policy and its relative ability to help prevent attacks and to defend against them if they occur. Those efforts, therefore, must be separated from ex-positions of the assertions of the total convictions of individuals or the comprehensive political perspective or world view of organizations. Those will, appropriately, be expounded on other occasions and in different contexts. There is room for people and groups with differing beliefs and various broader insights and programs to con-sider the potential of civilian-based defense.

We need to approach the efforts to gain wider attention and con-sideration of this policy with the attitude that we all have much to learn. Also, our efforts need to be of the highest quality possible to contribute to maximum effectiveness.

Some steps toward consideration and evaluation of civilian-based defense can only be taken at more advanced stages, which have been reached in a few European countries. In the United States, Canada, most European countries, and elsewhere, however, the basic steps in investigation and exploration need to be the primary activities to lay a sound foundation for more ambitious later steps.

Each of these steps produces positive gains, extending and deepening the understanding of nonviolent alternatives in the socie-ty. However small any particular steps may seem, they are nonetheless gains which contribute to long-term lasting changes.

The following are among the steps which may be taken:

1. *Self-education and thought* by individuals and groups already in-terested. Individual study and study groups to gain both a basic in-troduction and an in-depth understanding are highly important. These will prepare people to be able to evaluate for themselves this policy proposal, and, if they find it important, to be more effective in future steps to spread information and promote consideration of the policy. *This step is basic.*

2. *Informal public educational efforts* include a variety of specific tasks:

   A. Promotion and sale of pamphlets and books on civilian-based defense, and encouragement of libraries to make them available. Titles of basic items are listed in the "For Further Reading" section.

B. Promotion and use of the videotape series "Alternatives to Violence" for meetings, discussion groups, and the like, and encouraging cable and educational television stations to broadcast them. (These are funded by the U.S. Department of Education.) Enquiries about the programs, and sales and lease of tapes, should be send to: W.T.L. (Distribution), Box 351, Primos, Pennsylvania 19018.

C. With quality material and skillful approaches by informed persons, newspapers may sometimes be persuaded to publish articles on civilian-based defense, review books on the policy, or call attention to pamphlets about it. Reporters will sometimes prepare stories on meetings and lectures, and interview speakers visiting the city or campus. Occasionally, feature articles or op ed pieces may be accepted, either original ones or excerpts or reprints of existing publications.

D. In connection with conferences and visiting lecturers, radio and television stations will often broadcast short or feature interviews with specialists on civilian-based defense.

E. Discussion meetings and study groups aimed at persons previously unfamiliar with the policy — both with appropriate readings — may be organized. These may aim to reach the general public, or primarily members of the sponsoring organization, such as international relations and foreign policy groups, unions, churches, peace groups, defense policy bodies, and political organizations and parties.

F. The holding of special lectures for the general public and on campuses (perhaps in combination with other activities).

G. On occasion, given the receptivity and wise and careful planning, one- to two-day conferences on civilian-based defense may be effective. These may be primarily addressed to the general public, students and faculty, or people with particular interests. Diverse viewpoints need to be presented.

3. *Personal development of skills* for future work on civilian-based defense may be important in the long-run development and consideration of the policy. In addition to in-depth self-education, persons may seek to improve their capacities as public speakers and writers, for example, in making contacts with various organizations and the media, and in becoming future researchers and analysts.

4. *Formal educational courses and programs,* at all ages and levels, may be important in conveying information and encouraging thought about alternatives to violence, even in the field of national defense. Sometimes this material can be included within existing courses — as attention to nonviolent struggles as part of events in a

period of history — and at other times new courses of various possible types may be introduced. The aim of these is not to gain converts, of course, but to spread information and understanding, and to stimulate students to think for themselves about these and other options. Teachers' guides and workshops may be helpful in this work. Videotapes and reading material mentioned elsewhere can be of assistance here also.

5. *Money to finance* research, analysis, and preparation of educational resources is urgently needed, since the established foundations never include nonviolent alternatives as a program to which they allocate funds for grants.

6. *Local, state, and national organizations* might establish special commissions or committees to study and evaluate civilian-based defense with a view to determining whether or not it merits their continued attention and inclusion in the areas of concern of the body. The types of organizations which might set up such study bodies include foreign policy and international relations groups, defense policy groups, councils or churches, individual denominations and religious groups, trade unions, organizations of educators, and political groups and parties (Republican, Democratic, and other).

The above six steps, carried out thoroughly and effectively, will provide the necessary groundwork for later larger-scale steps toward consideration and evaluation of civilian-based defense. Also highly important are new studies of the nature of nonviolent struggle, strategies and problems of civilian-based defense, the nature of threats against which the policy might have to operate, and various related fields. Such research and policy studies will greatly assist educational work and public consideration of the policy.

The combination of the basic steps in information and exploration and, at more advanced stages, the steps toward consideration and evaluation will prepare the way for a new stage. That is the explicitly political consideration and evaluation of the capacities, problems, merits, and potential of civilian-based defense in comparison with existing and other optional policies. Then a variety of steps in consideration become possible: state and federal appropriations for research and policy studies, committee hearings in the House of Representatives and Senate, working bodies within the Department of Defense and Department of State, and perhaps other federal departments, consideration and action on the local and state governmental levels, establishment of one or more privately organized "alternative defense commissions" with highly competent and respected participants, and other measures. A variety of preparatory and accompanying grass roots activities may be required in those connections. In other countries the political steps would differ somewhat.

All this is, of course, still prefatory to the first steps toward adding a civilian-based defense component alongside existing military capacities, and to the more advanced stages of the transarmament process.

In the case of the United States it is almost inevitable that the democratic societies now allied with the U.S. would need to develop an adequate self-defense capacity, as through civilian-based defense, before the U.S. would take significant steps toward reliance on civilian-based defense itself on the international level. It could, however, fairly early share research, policy studies, and technical information with countries exploring the policy or adding a civilian-based defense component. It could also add this capacity to defend against *coups d'état* or presidential usurpations.

Some countries are already much more advanced than this. Sweden is already preparing a plan for the use of nonmilitary resistance as part of its total — predominantly military — defense policy.

It is envisaged that generally the transarmament process would be a gradual, phased, development, building up the civilian-based defense component as a consequence of a series of decisions on whether to continue or to expand it, made through the normal democratic procedures. As the roles of non-governmental organizations would be highly important in the waging of civilian-based defense struggles, it would be important that they participate fully in the activities of the information and exploration stage, and also of the period of consideration and development. When a decision is made to add a civilian-based component to the defense policy, the involvement of those organizations and institutions would be essential.

In the advanced stages of consideration of this defense policy, under special circumstances those organizations might exercise more initiative in decision-making. If the democratic procedures were blocked at the point at which the society was ready to begin the transarmament process, churches, professional organizations, unions, business groups, educational institutions, and many others might independently determine that in case of internal usurpation or foreign invasion their members would be expected and prepared to refuse collaboration and to participate in civilian-based defense of the country's constitution and independence.

The nongovernmental organizations might, therefore, be supportive of an official transarmament decision, operate parallel to it, or even provide leadership for defense in cases where the goverment had been unable or unwilling to do so.

Much sharing of information, encouragement of thought, consideration, and evaluation — all on top of research and policy studies — will be required from the initial points of the introduction of the concept to the implementation of a decision to transarm. Great sensitivity and sound political judgement will be required to determine when the important groundwork has been adequately prepared to enable responsible and durable more ambitious steps to be taken in the further consideration and evaluation of the potential of civilian-based defense.

KEY DEFINITIONS

CIVILIAN-BASED DEFENSE . . .

Civilian-based defense is an alternative policy which uses nonmilitary forms of struggle, either as a supplement to military means, or as a full alternative to them to deter and defend a society against attacks.

This policy has also variously been called "civilian-based defense," "social defense," "nonmilitary defense," and "nonviolent defense."

The term "civilian-based defense" indicates defense by civilians (as distinct from military personnel) using civilian means of struggle (as distinct from military and paramilitary means). Civilian-based defense is a policy intended to deter and defeat foreign military invasions, occupations, and internal usurpations. The last includes *coups d'état* — with or without foreign instigation and aid.

Deterrence and defense are to be accomplished by civilian forms of struggle — social, economic, political, and psychological. These are used to wage widespread noncooperation and to offer massive public defiance. The aim is to deny the attacker his desired objectives, and also to make impossible the consolidation of foreign rule, a puppet regime, or a government of usurpers.

This noncooperation and defiance is also combined with other forms of action intended to subvert the loyalty of the attacker's troops and functionaries and to promote their unreliability in carrying out orders and repression, and even to secure their mutiny.

Civilian-based defense measures are designed to be applied by the general population, the particular population groups most affected by the attacker's objectives and actions, and by the institutions of the society. Which of these are most involved varies with the attacker's aims — whether they are economic, ideological, political or other.

Civilian-based defense is meant to be waged, on the basis of advance preparations, planning, and training, by the population and members of institutions. Preparations and training would be based upon the findings of basic research into these types of resistance and into the systems of the attacker, and upon intensive problem-solving research. The latter needs to focus on ways to improve the effectiveness of such resistance, to meet impediments, and to solve problems in its application, especially against ruthless regimes. Understanding of the requirements for effectiveness of these forms of struggle and of the ways to aggravate weaknesses of the attacker's system and regime is the foundation for developing successful strategies of civilian-based defense.

DEFENSE IS. . .

Defense is action which preserves, protects, or maintains an individual, group, society, or country against hostile attack. Defense is also the goal of such protection, minimizing of harm, and preservation. All action taken with the intent of defending against attack does not produce the same result.

Applied to a whole country, defense means the protection or preservation of a country's independence, its right to choose its own way of life, institutions, and standards of legitimacy, and the protection to the maximum degree possible of its own people's lives, freedoms, and opportunities for future development.

Defense is contrasted to offense and attack. Such actions as invading or bombing another country, or arranging a *coup d'état* against its government, would not be "defense" but "attack."

Military means are recognized as the predominant methods used to provide defense throughout history. However, defense and military means are not synonymous. Both conceptually and in practice they are distinct; defense is the objective, the result, or action which is actually protecting against attack while military action is one set of means (among possible others) which may be intended to achieve defense or other goals and which may or may not do so.

In certain situations military means have been incapable of actually defending, as distinct from attacking, combatting, or retaliating, or have produced only destruction. On the other hand, defense has sometimes been provided by nonmilitary means, by noncooperation and other improvised civilian struggle.

DETERRENCE IS. . .

Deterrence is the process of restraining or preventing a potential attacker from committing an aggressive or hostile act by convincing him that such an act would prove to be unacceptably costly for the attacker. Deterrence is thus a much broader concept than military or nuclear deterrence. It may also be a particular factor contributing to dissuasion.

While military means have been widely recognized as useful for deterrence, they are not the only possibilities. At times deterrence against international aggression may instead be provided by the prepared capacity of the population to resist the military occupation which usually follows invasions, for example. That resistance capacity might be expressed by guerrilla warfare or by nonmilitary means of resistance and defiance. Deterrence might also be achieved by a credible threat by third parties to impose intolerable economic sanctions in event of attack.

The punishment capacity which can produce deterrence may, therefore, be achieved not only by ability to destroy and kill but also by ability to deny something needed or seriously desired by the potential attacker and to produce other serious undesired consequences for the attacker. This punishment may be achieved by violent or nonviolent means.

DISSUASION IS. . .

Dissuasion is inducement of a person, group, or government not to carry out a course of action which had been considered or planned, especially a contemplated hostile action. Influences leading to dissuasion may include rational argument, moral appeal, alteration of the situation, distraction, adoption of an unoffending policy, and deterrence in the broad sense. Dissuasion is a broader concept than deterrence.

NATIONAL SECURITY IS. . .

National security is the condition in which a nation or country is safe from attack.

National security may occur because there are no dangers, but that situation is rare in the modern world. It is more likely to be the result of dissuasion of potential attackers, either by means which cause them no longer to wish to launch hostile activities or by detterence of some means so that while still hostile they nevertheless wish to avoid the consequences of any contemplated attack.,

When national security is violated by actual attack, effective means to defend against the attack and to protect the citizenry as best possible are required. The defense objective is to end the assault and restore the society's independence of action and condition of safety.

The choice of means to do this is highly important. Some means intended for defense may themselves pose the threat or probability of massive destruction of the attacked society in the effort to save it. Other forms may provide maximum defensive capacity with minimal injury to the country and its people. In addition to the means of defense, other measures and policies may contribute to national security by contributing to dissuasion of potential attackers or to the internal resilience of the society which would increase its defense motivation and capacity if attacked.

National security, as viewed here, is thus not identified with ability to secure from other parts of the world all desired economic resources on one's own terms, nor with capacity to control the economies, politics, and military actions of other countries and to intervene militarily throughout the world. Indeed, such ability and capacity are likely in the long run to produce hostile reactions and therefore insecurity for the country which has attempted that type of world role.

The plea of "national security" to justify internal repression and violation of civil liberties is also inconsistent with the usage recommended here. To the contrary, such measures are attacks on the society's security under a democratic constitutional system.

NONVIOLENT ACTION IS. . .

Nonviolent action is a technique of conducting protest, resistance, and intervention without physical violence by: (a) acts of omission (that is, the participants refuse to perform acts which they usually perform, are expected by custom to perform, or are required by law or regulation to perform); or (b) acts of commission (that is, the participants perform acts which they usually do not perform, are not expected by custom to perform, or are forbidden by law or regulation from performing); or (c) a combination of both.

The technique includes a multitude of specific methods which are grouped into three main classes: nonviolent protest and persuasion, noncooperation, and nonviolent intervention.

Nonviolent action may be used to wage active struggle and as a sanction in conflict situations where in its absence submission or violence might have been practiced.

Considerable variation exists within the technique, including the specific methods applied, the motivation for nonviolent behavior, the attitude toward the opponent, the objectives of the action, the intended mechanisms of change, and the relation of types of nonviolent action to other techniques of action.

The broad phenomenon of nonviolent action has variously been referred to, in part or in full, by such terms as "nonviolent resistance," "satyagraha," "passive resistance," "positive action," "nonviolent direct action," and "civil resistance." "Civilian struggle" indicates the application of nonviolent action.

The use of the term "nonviolent action" in contradistinction to "violent action," as the two main classes of ultimate sanctions, should not be interpreted as implying a dichotomy of all social and political action into "violent" and "nonviolent." Between them may be classed such broad categories as "simple verbal persuasion and related behavior," "peaceful institutional procedures backed by threat and use of sanctions (violent and nonviolent)," and "material destruction only."

TRANSARMAMENT IS. . .

Transarmament is the process of change-over from one weapons system to a fundamentally different one, especially from conventional military means or nuclear capacity to civilian-based defense.

The transarmament process would in most cases operate over an extended time period of some years during which the civilian-based defense capacity would be introduced as a component of the total defense policy, gradually built up and expanded, and, eventually, the military components phased down and replaced. In some cases a society might not transarm fully, but retain both military and civilian-based components in some combination.

Transarmament always involves the replacement of one means to provide defense with another, and not, as with disarmament, the simple reduction or abandonment of military capacity.

FOR FURTHER READING

On Nonviolent Struggle

Gene Sharp, *The Politics of Nonviolent Action,* 902 pp. Boston: Porter Sargent,* 1973. Paperback in three volumes: I, *Power and Struggle,* 105 pp.; II, *The Methods of Nonviolent Action,* 339 pp.; III, *The Dynamics of Nonviolent Action,* 457 pp. Boston: Porter Sargent, 1974.

On Civilian-Based Defense

Brigadier General Edward B. Atkeson, "The Relevance of Civilian-based Defense to U.S. Security Interests," *Military Review* (Fort Leavenworth, Kansas), vol. 56, no. 5, May 1976, pp. 24-32 and no. 6, June 1976, pp. 45-55.

Anders Boserup and Andrew Mack, *War Without Weapons.* New York: Schocken, + 1975. London: Francis Pinter, 1974.

Robert Irwin, "U.S. Defense Policy: Mainstream Views and Non-violent Alternatives" A study manual with readings**

Adam Roberts, ed., *Civilian Resistance as a National Defense.* Harrisburg: Stackpole Books,° 1968. English title: *The Strategy of Civilian Defence.* London: Faber, 1967.

---

* Porter Sargent Publishers, 11 Beacon Street, Boston, Massachusetts 02108.
+ Schocken Books, 200 Madison Ave., New York City, N.Y. 10016.
** Association for Transarmament Studies, 3636 Lafayette St., Omaha, Nebraska 68131.
° Stackpole Books, Cameron and Kelker Streets, Harrisburg, Pennsylvania 17105. The book is presently out of print but it may be reprinted.

Gene Sharp, *Exploring Nonviolent Alternatives.* Boston: Porter Sargent, 1970. Out of print, but often in libraries. See "Research Areas on Nonviolent Alternatives," pp. 73-113.

————, *Making Europe Unconquerable: The Potential of Civilian-based Deterrence and Defence** Includes an extensive multi-language bibliography. London and Philadelphia: Taylor and Francis, 1985.

————, "Making the Abolition of War a Realistic Goal" (pamphlet). 16 pp. Wallach Award Essay. New York: Institute for World Order, 1981.

————, "'The Political Equivalent of War' — Civilian-based Defense" and *"Seeking a Solution to the Problem of War"* in Gene Sharp, *Social Power and Political Freedom.* pp. 195-261 and 263-284. Boston: Porter Sargent, 1980.

Of Related Interest

Gene Sharp, "Gandhi's Defense Policy," and "Gandhi as a National Defense Strategist," in Gene Sharp, *Gandhi as a Political Strategist,* pp. 131-169 and 171-198. Boston: Porter Sargent, 1979.

————, "The Lesson of Eichmann," "Facing Dictatorships With Confidence," "The Societal Imperative," and "Popular Empowerment," in Gene Sharp, *Social Power and Political Freedom,* pp. 69-90, 91-112, 285-308, and 309-378. Boston: Porter Sargent, 1980.

Video Tapes

The first video tapes on nonviolent alternatives for educational use are now available: *Alternatives to Violence: Video Forum,* funded by The Fund for the Improvement of Postsecondary Education, United States Department of Education, through the University City Science Center, Philadelphia. Enquiries to: W.T.L. (Distribution), Box 351, Primos, Pennsylvania 19018.

---

*Taylor and Francis, Inc. 242 Cherry Street, Philadelphia, PA 19106 and Taylor and Francis, Ltd., 4 John Street, London WC1N2ET, England.
#Princeton University Press, Princeton, New Jersey 08540.

Audiotapes

"A Modern Alternative to War," Common Ground Tape #8324. Also, "More on Civilian-based Defense," Common Ground Tape #8440. $5.00 per each half-hour cassette, The Stanley Foundation, 420 East Third Street, Muscatine, Iowa 52761.

"Making Europe Unconquerable." $7.00 per half-hour cassette. Cambridge Forum, 3 Church Street, Cambridge, Massachusetts 02138.

RESEARCH AREAS
AND POLICY STUDIES
ON CIVILIAN-BASED DEFENSE

Exploration of the potential effectiveness of civilian-based defense requires a vast amount of research, analysis, and policy studies. These are needed to determine whether or not the assumptions of this policy are valid, and whether the difficult problems involved in its operation can be solved, and if so how. This information would contribute to an improved ability to evaluate the policy of civilian-based defense as such, and to determine whether or not it merits further attention. If so, such research would help to establish the types of situations and areas in which it may be practicable, if adequately prepared. Further research and policy studies would also help in deciding the extent to which civilian-based defense may be suitable in a supplementary capacity, in addition to military defense, and whether civilian-based defense may provide, as it has been designed, a full effective replacement for military means.

The areas suggested here are listed without reference to particular academic disciplines. Often an area or a specific problem may be examined from the perspective of more than one discipline, such as psychology, social psychology, history, political science, and sociology. Some problems, or topics within a problem area, might be explored with aid from the fields of education (especially adult education), anthropology, social ethics, and communications. Scholars in all disciplines are invited to examine these suggested problem areas, and to add to those offered, which are by no means definitive.

The areas for research and policy studies are grouped here into five broad fields: (1) the nature of the threats for which defense may be needed; (2) civilian-based defense: problems of adoption, politics, and practice; (3) the technique of nonviolent action; (4) internal use of nonviolent action; and (5) implications and consequences of nonviolent alternatives. Each particular area within those five fields is itself very broad; many individual research topics might be developed under each. Professional academics, graduate students, trained individuals, and undergraduates can all make contributions toward these studies.

THE NATURE OF THREATS
FOR WHICH DEFENSE MAY BE NEEDED

1. *Examination of the nature and needs of defense:*

Before rational examination is possible of the needs of defense and the possible viability of alternative means of meeting those needs, basic re-examination of the meaning of the term "defense" is required. It has come to be used with so many meanings that clarity of thought is impossible until these are separated, and the differing needs, tasks, perceptions, and objectives are distinguished. Attention is also needed to the differing functions which war and other military action have served and do at present, as well as separation of offensive and defensive purposes of military action, and the problems of misperception or misrepresentation concerning these among the civilian population. If defense needs are seen to include preservation both of national independence from foreign attack and occupation and of the legitimate, popularly accepted, regime from minority internal attack and overthrow, then means of effective defense are needed against both foreign and internal attacks — a broader perspective than is common among advocates of military defense.

2. *Coup d'état as internal usurpation:*

The large number of cases in which constitutional and other regimes have been overthrown by internal *coup d'état* (with or without foreign support) underlines the importance of defense against such threats and of research attention to the potential role of a civilian-based defense policy, in defeating them. Past experiences and existing studies of the phenomenon need to be examined with a view to predicting possible lines of action by such a usurping group, the vulnerable points and periods in such *coups*, the types of forces and conditions which may weaken or strengthen resistance to such an internal attack, and various possible strategies which might be employed against internal usurpation. Attention would also be required to the possibilities of new types of *coups* which might arise in countries with civilian-based defense policies, such as a *coup* in the change-over period by supporters of military defense, or actions attempted later by tiny fanatical groups which might estimate the country to be vulnerable even to them.

3. *Gradual erosion or abdication of constitutional government:*

The established constitutional system is sometimes destroyed gradually or officially, rather than by a quick stroke, as in a *coup*. Increasing suppression of civil liberties, growth of police and administrative powers, reduced effective legislative controls over the executive, by-passing or suspension of constitutional provisions, and even direct surrender by the legislature of its powers to the executive — as in the Enabling Act in Germany in 1933 — are illustrations of stages in which a phased destruction of constitutional government occurs. Attention is vitally needed also to the social conditions under which these changes occur and are accepted by the populace, such as a growth of internal violence and chaos within the country perhaps combined with international crises. Clearly at such times if the constitutional system is to be defended it requires support from the citizenry. Work is therefore needed to shed light on the conditions in which this threat occurs and is successful, and to the means of civilian defense of the constitutional system which may then be effectively applied.

4. *Guerrilla warfare as usurpation:*

Examination is needed as to 1) whether a country with a prepared civilian-based defense policy would be vulnerable to attempted minority usurpation in the form of guerrilla warfare or related terrorization of the population intended to produce noncooperation with, and the collapse of, the legitimate government; and 2) if so, what types of nonviolent strategies, tactics, and methods might be most appropriate in meeting such attempted guerrilla usurpation. Further, study would be needed to examine whether in the absence of advance preparations a country already under guerrilla attack could, by civilian-based defense measures, defeat the guerrillas by noncooperation and refusal to become terrorized into submission.

5. *Blockades as limited foreign attack:*

Certain countries or other political units are, because of their geography, size, and economy, especially vulnerable to external pressures by land, sea, or air blockades, or a combination of them. Britain and West Berlin are two obvious examples, but there are many others. If a hostile foreign regime were successfully deterred from military invasion by the civilian-based defense country's resistance capacity, the frustrated regime might seek to use its military forces to make the threatened country surrender or grant certain demands by imposing a blockade. This would be especially serious when it could drastically affect the supply of food and the economy. Or blockades might be imposed in quite different contexts, as the famous Berlin Blockade. The question then arises whether, and if so how, measures compatible with civilian-based defense could be used to break the blockade, and what might be done within the blockaded country to help it withstand the pressures. The Berlin experience and the successful airlift of food without military exchanges would be a case for study, but attention would be needed to quite different situations and varying types of blockades.

6. Invasions:

Conventional military invasions still occur, sometimes alone, and sometimes combined with another type of usurpation or attack, such as a foreign-supported *coup*. Conventional military defense forces are primarily designed to deal with foreign invasions; indeed, this capacity has historically been their final justification. It is for this type of attack that civilian-based defense was originally primarily developed, and for which it remains especially suitable. Research is needed in the varying forms which invasions may take, and the differing objectives for which they may be launched. These are highly important in formulating effective civilian-based defense measures, for the resistance should be able to thwart the attacker's objectives. Although minor delaying actions against the incursions of foreign troops and functionaries may be possible, civilian-based defense for various reasons does not attempt to halt such entry, and cannot successfully do so; the emphasis instead is on making the populace ungovernable by the foreign invaders. Problems of perception of intention and capacity therefore exist for everyone concerned, and research on them is needed. Diverse other research problems concerning invasions may arise, including the previous relationships between the countries, the balances of populations, economic power and the like, political outlooks and ideologies of the countries, differences where there is more than one invader, particular problems where the objective is highly limited, in contrast to complete reconstruction of the society of the invaded country and ideological conversion of its population. These are simply illustrative of the many specific topics requiring attention within this area.

7. Bombings of civilian-based defense countries:

There are conflicting opinions on the possibility that countries adopting civilian-based defense would be bombed. According to one view, a foreign enemy recognizing the immense problems of ruling a country with civilian-based defense might simply seek to impose its will on the country or remove this peculiar type of threat by destroying its cities or other important points with conventional or nuclear bombs, either on a progressive or periodic basis, or in one all-out attack. Proponents of the opposite view hold that there would be virtually no possibility at least of a nuclear attack against a country which had neither nuclear nor conventional military capacities. Between the extremes there are those who feel that, under certain conditions at least, such bombings might well take place, and that hence civilian defense presumes pre-nuclear Second World War conditions and has no relevance in today's world. In any case, a variety of strategic military and political factors would be involved for the attacking country. For the country with civilian-based defense, several research problems invite attention, including examination of measures which could reduce the chances of attack, alternative responses to threatened nuclear blackmail, methods of encouraging internal rebellion against the threatening regime at home, and ways to carry on if bombing threats were carried out. Examination is also required of the validity of the various views on the possibility of bombings under these conditions.

8. *The nature and weaknesses of totalitarian and other dictatorships:*

Resistance to a possible dictatorial enemy requires that the enemy must be known well, not only in terms of his ideology, objectives, and obvious strengths, but in terms of his inadequacies, weaknesses, vulnerable points and the like, in short, his Achilles' heels. There is much evidence that extreme dictatorships are often much weaker and more fragile than they are believed to be. Knowledge of these general features and specific characteristics of a particular system may be highly important in determining the appropriate strategy for resisting and undermining it.

9. *Genocide and other mass killings:*

Repeatedly in human history mass killings of unwanted people have occurred. The Nazi Holocaust of Jews, Gypsies, and Eastern Europeans has been followed by other large-scale slaughters in Kampuchea (Cambodia) and Africa. Modern technological, political, and biological developments make such atrocities more possible in the future than they were in the past. No effective means have yet been developed for preventing and defeating attempts at genocide, and evidence exists that war and other political violence may in fact facilitate genocide.

Some evidence from the Holocaust indicates that noncooperation by victims, the general population, enforcement officials, government personnel, and others significantly saved lives. Basic research, problem-solving research, and policy studies are urgently required to (1) develop ways to prevent attempts to commit genocide from being carried out in the first place, and (2) to defeat such attempts once initiated.

In particular, studies of the effects of various past responses and modes of resistance to genocide are needed, with special attention to violent and nonviolent resistance. The roles of foreign intervention and autonomous internal opposition both in the past and their potential for the future also require investigation. The roles of various groups and institutions in perpetrating genocide and in resisting it need investigation, along with examination of the potential of those bodies for future defense against genocide. The effects of a prepared civilian-based defense capacity on the prevention of genocide and opposition to it are a new element requiring analysis. These are only illustrative of other important aspects requiring study and policy development.

10. Nuclear and other weapons of mass destruction:
The new capacity, which emerged during and since the Second World War, for massive destruction and rapid decimation of many millions of people continues to expand. It threatens the existence of life as we know it. Diverse efforts to bring that capacity under control and to begin to dismantle it have failed to date.

While those efforts continue, new explorations are required of other possible ways to control and reverse the development of this capacity. It is necessary to examine, for example, whether this is possible within the context of military means. Or, would transarmament to civilian-based defense provide a way to reduce the likelihood of nuclear (and comparable) attacks while increasing actual defense capacity against foreign conventional invasions and occupations? Could a series of cases of partial and full transarmament by individual countries provide the self-reliance in security which some countries have sought by development of nuclear weapons? Are there merits in combining civilian-based defense for national security with serious civil defense to reduce casualties in case of unprovoked or accidental conventional or nuclear attack? What other options may exist, and what are the weaknesses and potentials of each?

11. Presidential defiance of constitutional limitations:
With the President as Commander-in-Chief of the military forces, and head of the executive branch which includes the F.B.I.,

C.I.A., and other bodies, it is highly important that the President comply with and submit to constitutional limits on his authority.

If for whatever reason (mental instability, political ambition, a sense of superior judgement, or whatever) he should violate those limits, the system would be in jeopardy. He might, for example, defy a clear Supreme Court ruling that he should or should not do a certain thing. He might refuse to leave office when impeached by Congress (or might even refuse to allow the impeachment proceedings to be held). He might call upon the police and military forces to back him against the rest of the government.

For such a major constitutional crisis there is no procedural remedy. The danger could be short-lived, but it could, even if not originally intended by the President, lead step-by-step to presidential usurpation. The danger could also take the much more limited form of a specific and defiant violation of the War Power Act (say, by sending U.S. troops to Taiwan, and defiantly refusing to bow to Supreme Court and Congressional judgements against such action). That could lead to a still more serious test of the viability of the Constitution.

While many actions might be taken to forestall such crises, the most serious problem is what to do in the extreme situation.

What options between civil war and acquiescence to the defiant President would the American system have in such situations? Would it be possible, and if so in what specific ways, to build remedies into the legal system, and into the conceptions of the rights and duties of the citizenry, the civil servants, the society's institutions, the military forces, police, etc.? What could constitute effective means of putting peaceful brakes on a runaway president, both to defend the integrity of the constitutional system and to minimize the dangers of bitterly splitting the country? How might some such means be incorporated into laws and then in the specific instance be determined to be required, and then implemented effectively?

CIVILIAN-BASED DEFENSE: PROBLEMS OF ADOPTION, POLITICS, AND PRACTICE

A. Adoption and basic operation

12. *Conceptions of nonviolent action in American society:*

If one is considering the possibility of trying to convince Americans that nonviolent action is a practical alternative to violence, or that a civilian-based defense policy could be a practical substitute for military defense, one would need to know more about present American views of these phenomena:

1) How do Americans conceive of nonviolent action? What is the extent of their knowledge and understanding? What do they think of when they hear or read the words "nonviolent resistance," "passive resistance," "nonviolent action," Gandhi, Martin Luther King, etc.?

2) What arguments do they offer in favor of the technique and against it?

3) Is there any conception at all, and if so what type, of the possibility of resisting by popular action a foreign occupation or attempted internal take-over?

4) Is there any more, or less, evidence of understanding of the phenomena themselves if differing terminologies are used in the investigations?

The second and third parts of this would require more than simply answering straight questions, the answers to which might be superficial or even inaccurate representations of the real attitude; in-depth interviews or some similar method would probably be required. It would be important to search for both "intellectual" and "emotional" reasons, as well as those possibly associated with sex roles. It is possible, but not certain, that these two objectives might be realizable with the same project. It would seem important that answers be sought to these questions among various sections of the populace to find out, for example, what differences may exist between intellectuals and nonintellectuals, urban and rural people, upper, middle, and lower classes, various ethnic and cultural groups, broad religious groups, and possibly parts of the country. Careful control of the samples chosen would be essential.

One or more pilot experiments might be provided to follow up the major studies in which given, previously interviewed subjects would be subjected to attempts to provide them with information attempting to answer their main objections or correct their misconceptions. They would then, after a time lapse, be interviewed again to determine what, if any, effect the effort had made. A control group would, of course, be necessary for effective validation of this study.

13. *Achieving understanding and acceptance of civilian-based defense:*

Even if the many practical problems involved in making civilian-based defense sufficiently effective to merit adoption in place of military defense can be solved, there remain a variety of obstacles to its acceptance among the general population; without such acceptance it could never work. Attention is therefore needed to the problems of overcoming both irrational and rational obstacles to it. Some of these are related to the problems discussed in the previous section, but others have to do entirely with civilian-based defense. In what ways can the assumed identification of defense with violence be altered? How can the historical distortions concerning the roles of violent and nonviolent action be corrected? Under what conditions will people be willing to participate in their own defense instead of leaving the matter to experts and professionals? How will a transition period, in which military defense will be phased down and eventually out only as civilian-based defense measures are well prepared, affect people's attitudes? What role is there for the assumed psychological propensity to violence? What knowledge relevant to adoption of civilian-based defense can be learned from past cases where people who normally had accepted military means have, for limited periods, used unprepared nonviolent resistance for national defense purposes? How do perceptions of nuclear weapons as deterrents affect possible attitudes to adoption of civilian-based defense? Are there psychological blocks to acceptance of a deterrence capacity by civilian-based defense preparations? These questions are only illustrative. Also important are questions of educational and political strategy for gaining acceptance and adoption of civilian-based defense.

14. *Political factors in civilian-based defense:*

As civilian-based defense is much more intimately associated with the political conditions of the defending country than is military defense, serious attention is required to what political conditions may be required for, or most suitable for, effective civilian-based defense measures. Various questions arise here, of which these are only suggestive. Is there a minimal degree of popular participation in government required for this policy? Is a considerable degree of political decentralization required or not? Is a particular degree of formal political education among the population required? Can civilian-based defense be adapted for newly-independent countries? What are the differences in the conditions for the operation of the defense policy between various types of countries (thinly and densely populated, large, medium, and small, various types of terrain and climates)? Could civilian-based defense make possible greater degrees of democracy within the country itself? What of the possible role of either indirect influences or direct efforts to encourage the liberalization or disintegration of dictatorial foreign and domestic regimes as a contribution to reduced incidence of international conflict and aggression? Is there an intrinsic connection between democratic political systems and the requirements for popular participation in civilian-based defense struggle, or not?

15. *The change-over period, training and preparations:*

The transarmament to civilian-based defense would require not only vast advance research and planning, but immense programs of training the population in how to conduct such resistance, and otherwise preparing for these eventualities. These other preparations might include a large variety of steps, such as provision of material supplies, means of communication, food supplies, etc. In addition, there would be a difficult transition period of some years between full dependence on military defense and full dependence on civilian-based defense while these preparations and training were being carried out and the country was increasing its civilian "combat strength" to the point where it was felt possible to abandon the military element. These extraordinarily complex problems require very careful and full examination.

16. *Cultural survival and foreign rule:*

There have been a number of instances in which extended foreign occupation and rule has resulted in one of two extremes: the elimination of an identifiable, distinct culture of the conquered population; or the survival of the culture in face of these conditions for hundreds of years. What are the important causal factors which facilitate or prevent cultural survival and what are the roles of linguistic, religious, cultural, and social factors in this phenomenon? Individual and comparative studies of such cases might shed important light on the conditions under which it is possible for a people to preserve its way of life under the most adverse conditions.

17. *Dissuasive and deterrent effects:*

It is, of course, desirable not to be attacked in the first place, so as not to be required to apply actual defensive struggle. A major claim for both conventional and nuclear weaponry is that they can deter attack. As nonviolent struggle for national defense has never been prepared in advance and the population trained before the crisis in how to wage it, there is little or no historical evidence for the deterrent and broader dissuasive effects of civilian-based defense. Investigation is required into the potential of this policy for preventing attacks.

Work is needed on identifying and evaluating the influences of the factors which may dissuade or deter a potential attacker. These seem to fall roughly into two categories: those which influence the hostile regime not to want to attack, and those which convince the regime that, although it would like to attack, the venture would likely fail and result in losses and costs it does not wish to suffer.

In the first category, to what degree in specific instances would the absence of an offensive military and nuclear capacity, and bases for them, make the country nondangerous and hence an inappropriate target? What influence might positive policies accompanying or following transarmament have on reducing animosities or strengthening goodwill so as to reduce the likelihood of attack?

In the second category, would both the real defense capacity of the society, and the potential attacker's perception of it, be sufficient to convince him that the desired goals of the attack could not be achieved and that the problems of controlling and ruling the prepared defiant population would be insurmountable? The costs might include the difficulties of controlling the population which had tried to make itself politically indigestible, potential opposition to the venture at home, possible disaffection in its own administration, police, and military occupation forces, and international political and economic repercussions. Or, despite a potential strong defense capacity, might the potential attacker perceive only weakness and hence be encouraged by the abandonment of military means to attack? In addition to problems of perception, all factors related to the actual defense capacity of a society which has adopted civilian-based defense would require consideration.

18. *Occupation policies and measures:*

It would be foolhardy to concentrate all research attention on possible actions of the civilian defenders. One must focus attention also on the types of occupation policies and measures which have been used in the past by international aggressors and empires in efforts to subdue and rule the conquered territories and their populaces. Particular attention should be directed to recent developments, some possible innovations in such policies and measures, and to possible future developments. These studies will provide suggestive insights into the kinds of situations and measures which the civilian defenders may have to face.

19. *Forms for resistance organizations:*

Under conditions of severe repression and dictatorial or totalitarian controls the problems of operating an organized resistance movement become serious. That organized resistance has happened in the past, however, proves that these obstacles are not insuperable, although they do require both research into how these were dealt with in past cases and examination of possible innovations which might be of use in future emergencies. In addition to problems of structure and day-to-day communication within the movement and with the general population, attention will be needed to the degree to which the actual organization can or cannot be set up in advance of the usurpation and the degree to which unstructured or spontaneous mass actions may play a role. (In the latter actions, the population would act on the basis of pre-determined plans which would operate in the case of given anticipated events even if a separate resistance organization were unable to act because of arrests, etc.) Various other factors in relation to organization need examination, including the roles of neighborhood and occupational groupings, religious and political bodies, i.e., the normal institutional structure of the society.

20. *Stragegy and tactics of civilian-based defense:*

The field of strategy and tactics in civilian-based defense is at least as complex as in conventional military defense, and may be even more so, as the combatants are likely to consist of nearly the full population of the transarmed country and virtually all of the organizations and institutions of that country are likely to be involved. Attention will be needed, first, to general principles of strategy and tactics in nonviolent action as a political technique of struggle; this will require examination of past strategies and tactics. Possible innovations in general types may be considered in light of the dynamics and mechanisms of nonviolent action.

But in addition to such general principles, attention will be needed to possible alternative strategies and tactics to meet a large variety of specific types of situations, as influenced by such factors as the country or part of the country threatened, the nature of the internal or foreign usurper (including his ideology, sources of power, means of repression and other influence), the objectives of the opponent, and his possible strategies and tactics. It would be important to work out systematically a considerable variety of strategic and tactical responses to various kinds of stages of attack as well as to develop the stages and measures by which one goes from strictly defensive action to offensive action in an attempt to disintegrate the usurper's power and regime.

21. *Special questions of methods and tactics:*

Certain special problems in the waging of civilian-based defense struggles may require particular attention. The following are simply suggestive: What are the forms and effects, respectively, of full or selective social boycott, and of fraternization and other types of contact (without collaboration) with the personnel of the occupying forces? What role should the legitimate police play in resistance against an occupation or internal take-over? For example, should they resign, disappear, continue their legal duties but refuse illegitimate orders, pretend to collaborate but be inefficient (lose records, warn persons to escape before attempting arrests, be unable to locate wanted persons, etc.), seek to arrest individuals of the occupation force or usurping regime? What capacity do armed forces and police units have for disciplined nonviolent action? This might be important in two types of situations: first, if civilian-based defense were initially adopted by a country for the limited purpose of dealing with a *coup d'état,* and second, if it were deemed desirable to keep together existing disciplined groups and teams, giving them new tasks for carrying out security duties. What should civil servants do in particular types of crises? Should they strike, engage in selective noncooperation, carry out legitimate policies only and "work-on," "lose" key records, etc.? If enemy armed forces occupy the capital, should the main governmental officials flee and maintain a new headquarters elsewhere in the country or abroad, or should they try to continue to carry out legitimate duties until arrested, or go underground as a basis for resistance and a parallel government in the country itself, or some combination of these, with perhaps different persons assigned to different roles? What is to be learned from past experience with parallel government which is relevant to civilian-based defense? What is the contribution of international economic sanctions against aggressors or usurpers generally, and especially in relation to support for attacked civilian-based defense countries? What is to be learned positively or negatively, from past international attempts at economic boycotts and embargoes, as against Mussolini's Italy, South Africa, and Rhodesia, and what are the conditions which must be met if they are to be most effective?

22. *Repression and other counteraction against nonviolent struggle:*

The enforcement problems against a group or population using nonviolent means of struggle are quite distinct from those arising in cases of general lawlessness or from some type of violent struggle. Experience has gradually begun to accumulate as a result of governmental, police, and military counter-measures; and it is certain that a group or regime seriously contemplating military usurpation against a civilian-based defense country would try not only to review this experience but also to devise innovations. It is therefore highly important that the civilian defenders themselves should be aware of these in some detail in order to be able to meet such measures and to prepare possible countering responses.

B. Special problems

23. *Possible combination of civilian-based defense with military defense, guerrilla warfare and sabotage:*
    While most exponents of civilian-based defense have recognized the inevitability of a period of transition in whch civilian-based defense preparations and military defense preparations would co-exist, considerable disagreement exists relative to the advisability of using such a combination in a permanent policy. On the one hand, some have advocated combining civilian-based defense with conventional military defense, so that the former would go into operation after the failure of the latter; others have advocated abandoning frontal military defense measures, but combining civilian-based defense with guerrilla warfare and/or sabotage measures, with different tasks being assigned to the different types of struggle. On the other hand, some theorists argue that although it seems immediately appealing to use all possible types of struggle in the attempt to get maximum total combat strength, the problem of the "mix" is not that simple. Instead, they contend, such a combination may destroy some highly important strategic advantages of civilian-based defense alone, and because the techniques possess quite different mechanisms and dynamics, the use of violent means may seriously interfere with or destroy the power-altering capacities of civilian-based defense struggle to seek to obtain the mutiny of the enemy's soldiers, or at least attain sufficient uncertainty or sympathy from them that that are deliberately inefficient in obeying orders; but if they and their friends are being shot at or killed, this possibility is enormously reduced. Because of the complexity of the problem of "the mix," it requires serious research and analysis.

24. *Cases of little or no dependence on the population:*
    In most types of usurpation, there is a considerable degree of dependence on the population of the country which has been seized, and hence a strong basis for opposition by noncooperation. However, in certain unusual types of aggression this is not the case; if civilian-based defense measures are to operate at all in such cases,

they must do so by quite different means. These situations are illustrated by military occupation of unpopulated mountainous or desert areas for such purposes, or international psychological effects; the seizure of a limited coastal area or port as a naval base (such as Gibraltar) without other attempts to control the country as a whole; or cases in which an invader would intend to deport or annihilate the entire original population and replace them by her own colonists.

25. *Technological developments of civilian-based defense:*

Modern developments in the technology of communication, transportation, police methods, as well as psychological manipulation, pose serious problems for civilian defense. Opposing views have been presented concerning these: Rapid communication and transportation clearly make it easier for a usurper to move against centers of resistance, but can technological developments also be used to assist the resisters? Transistorized broadcasting sets and radios are one small example. Are the influences of technological and scientific developments altered in any way by the type of nonviolent resistance used: whether it operates with complete openness and defiance; whether it attempts to operate on the basis of secrecy for a major part of its activities; whether a small group aims to remain in hiding directing operations; or whether the whole population knows what to do in various contingencies without further instructions, and the like? Investigation of these and many other problems is needed by people familiar with both civilian-based defense and communication developments.

26. *The roles of economic organization and industrial technology:*

Production and distribution systems are important in the conduct of civilian-based defense and for most rulers or occupation regimes. But since the social organization and the technology for these systems can differ so widely, these differences may produce diverse problems for civilian defense. Even for centralized industrial systems, opposite conclusions have been reached by those who have considered the problem; these conclusions range from the view that extreme agrarian decentralization is necessary for effective resistance, to the position that resistance is more effective in a centralized industrial system, since highly vulnerable key points may cause selective noncooperation to disrupt the whole system. Complex problems also relate to the degree of national self-sufficiency of the economy versus international economic interdependence. Automation introduces new factors into an already difficult problem area. Examination should also be made of types of economic noncooperation which might be most suitable against usurpers with a variety of political and economic objectives.

27. *Riots in civilian-based defense countries:*

Riots within a civilian-based defense country are possible under such conditions as the following: the existence of deep divisions within the country on political, economic, cultural, linguistic, or racial lines; the existence of a strong group intent on using violent means to obtain a restoration of military defense; the presence of a significant number of sympathizers with a hostile foreign power; widespread boredom among youths seeking excitement in non-political rioting. Various investigations of such rioting are required in relation to civilian-based defense; for example: determining effects of such rioting on civilian-based defense capacity; whether, and if so how, civilian-based defense preparations might include measures to reduce or prevent rioting; the nature and workings of both nonlethal and nonviolent means of controlling large crowds and halting rioting; examination of existing experience in the use of police and military means of riot control, and the relationship of such means to other factors.

C. Civilian-based defense for particular countries

28. *Pilot feasibility studies:*

Several plot projects should be undertaken to examine the feasibility of civilian-based defense in specific situations of relatively limited scope, against a particular type of threat. Such studies would involve extensive information about the assumed attacker, the defending country, and the international situation. It would be important to know the attacker's objectives, ideology, probable strategies and methods, international position, degree of internal stability and support, and possible explanations or justifications for his attempted usurpation. Knowledge required about the defending country or area would include: the social structure, political system and traditions; intensity of commitment to the society and principles being defended, the state and vitality of the economy, structure, composition and degree of dependence on external markets or supplies; the degree and type of presumed advance training for civilian-based defense and experience with nonviolent action; the communication and transportation systems: geographical characteristics; general and particular characteristics of population; and the like. Relevant international factors include: the degree of dependence of the usurper on other countries; the type, intensity and distribution of sympathies and attitudes throughout lthe world toward the defenders and usurpers; and the existence or absence of advance agreements and preparations for other countries and international bodies to offer various types of concrete assistance in such situations. Determination of specific forms of possible international assistance would also be important. These might include supplies, food, monetary aid, radio, printing, diplomatic assistance, economic sanctions against the usurper, refusal of recognition of the usurper and/or expulsion of his regime from international organizations, etc.

With this basic information, very concrete plans would need to be drawn up to meet the presumed usurpation, each considering possible alternative strategies and methods of resistance which might be most appropriate, in view of the factors previously examined, the opponent's possible and probable types of reaction and repression along with the means of countering these, the roles of resistance by the general population, as well as by specific occupational, age, or geographical groups and other specific factors.

Such pilot feasibility studies might be worked out to meet such situations as the following:

1) The defense of West Berlin against an attempted East German or Soviet military takeover

2) The defense of Norway against a conventional military attack and occupation, either by the Soviet Union or by some other power

3) The defense of Poland against a Soviet attack

4) The defense of civilian constitutional government against military or other *coups d'état* in Zambia, Tanzania, the Dominican Republic, Italy, or the United States

5) Resistance to attempts to impose minority one-party dictatorships by guerilla warfare, as in Costa Rica or India, including economic and political factors and specific means of noncooperation and refusal to submit to terrorism

6) Defense by a small Latin American country, such as Nicaragua, against U.S. political and military intervention in its internal affairs

29. *European security problems:*

Ever since the mid-1940s Western European countries and the U.S. government have been dubious of the capactiy of conventional military means to defend successfully Western Europe in case of a determined Soviet conventional military sweep toward the Channel. That doubt was related to the threat under John Foster Dulles of "massive retaliation" and the option of "first use," as it is today to the discussion of tactical nuclear weapons and the placing of new delivery systems. Soviet experience with the difficulties of ruling restive populations in Eastern Europe has been considerable. Civilian-based defense has been the most seriously explored in several Western European countries of any part of the world.

An examination of the potential role of civilian-based defense would require attention to such questions as these: What might be Soviet objectives in a sweep westward? Under what conditions might this occur? How can the various defense options be compared? What are the problems of existing policies? Would the prospective U.S. use of small nuclear weapons against advancing Soviet armies contribute to European resistance or to surrender?

What different defense problems and tasks would exist if a Soviet attack took the form of (1) the seizure of highly limited geographical objectives (for a submarine base), (2) military backing for an indigenous Communist party government, or (3) full occupation to achieve general military, economic, or political objectives requiring short-term or long-term military occupations.

Examination of the potential of civilian-based defense would include evaluation of existing experience in anti-Soviet civilian struggles without preparations, and examination of the possibility of deliberately increasing the effectiveness of future struggle as a consequence of research, analysis, training, strategic planning, national preparations prior to attack, and the like.

Attention would also be given to the potential of selective resistance, paralyzing noncooperation, and attempts to induce mutinies of Soviet troops or, those of another attacker. Other topics include: possible simultaneous unrest in Eastern Europe and among Soviet nationalities; further splits among the Communist parties of Western Europe; the roles of presently neutral countries; conditions for achieving a Soviet withdrawal; relationships with the United States and N.A.T.O.; and Soviet perceptions.

Attention would be required to the diverse possible patterns of European adoption of civilian-based defense, including:

(1) neutral countries — as Sweden and Austria — adopting civilian-based defense in part or in full; then civilian-based defense adopted as a secondary line of defense by certain N.A.T.O. countries — as the Netherlands, Belgium, Norway, and Denmark initially; then extension of civilian-based defense by such countries withdrawing from N.A.T.O. to adopt the policy fully; finally, establishment of a civilian-based defense-oriented European Treaty Organization to share research, plans, and information, and to provide mutual assistance in times of crisis; (2) an official N.A.T.O.-phased adoption, initially as a supplementary line of defense, gradually phasing civilian-based defense upward in importance to full transarmament; consideration of possible Soviet

nuclear threats and U.S. nuclear threats to the Soviet Union as possible and complicating developments; and (3) a negotiated phased disengagement of N.A.T.O. and Warsaw pact troops from middle Europe with a phased introduction of civilian-based defense simultaneously in several countries now in both alliances, aiming toward full substitution of civilian-based defense in them, creating a corridor between the military forces and bases of the U.S. and the U.S.S.R. (See the next section.)

Other aspects requiring attention would be the consequences of civilian-based defense on the degree of Western European self-reliance in defense; the appropriate forms of continuing U.S. involvement and assistance; and the impact on general U.S. international security policies.

Such conceptions and problems, along with many others, would require careful examination in problem-solving research and policy studies, often focussing on the needs and problems as applied to specific countries.

Attention to the dangers of *coups d'état* from diverse sources, military and political, with and without foreign involvement is also required as part of the consideration of civilian-based defense to European security problems.

30. *Civilian-based defense and disengagement of central Europe:*

Proposals for various types of disengagement in Central Europe to reduce East-West tension all have to face the question of how such countries would be expected to defend themselves, once American or Russian troops had been withdrawn, in case of foreign invasion or attempted minority take-overs, without setting off a major East-West war in the process. The existence of a self-reliant, effective defense capacity in Central Europe could facilitate a pulling back by both Russian and American armed forces, because their presence is now supported by fear. In non-Communist countries of the area, the fear is that without such forces they would be subject to Communist invasion or take-over; and in East European countries it is that without Russian forces they might again be victims of neo-Nazi German aggression. The possibilities of civilian defense would need to be examined and developed for specific cases, and its potentialities and problems would need to be compared with those of alternative defense policies, whether conventional military, paramilitary, or some combination of one or both of these (and their subtypes).

31. *U.S. government responses to transarmament:*

The growth of serious strategic attention to civilian-based defense, and past attempts to apply similar resistance against invasions and *coups* without training or preparations, make it possible that in the foreseeable future some country or countries will officially transarm after advance preparations and training. Candidates for the first such countries include Austria and Finland, but others are not to be excluded.

What would be the international consequences of such transarmament? How should the U.S. government respond? Would civilian-based defense increase or reduce the self-defense capacity of those countries? Would civilian-based defense dissuade, deter, or invite attack? Would such transarmament be compatible with, or threaten, U.S. objectives? Could such transarmament be welcomed, or even assisted by the U.S. for specific countries with which we might be allied, such as Japan? What future relationships between a transarmed country and the U.S. could develop? Would transarmament be perceived as a possible threat to U.S. policies? Would the U.S. want to invade an oil-producing country with a civilian-based defense policy in case of a new oil embargo, or a Japan in order to maintain bases or a military "presence" in that area of the world? What are possible foreign policy or international security gains from such transarmament cases?

In case of the outbreak of unplanned and civilian struggle against a new invasion (similar to Czechoslovakia in 1968), or a civilian uprising against a domestic dictatorship or a foreign occupation (similar to Poland in 1980-81), or a civilian-based offensive invasion (as Morocco vs. the Spanish Sahara in 1975), what should be the U.S. response? Why?

32. *Sharing know-how on civilian struggle against internal usurpations and foreign invasions*

Individual governments, an international body (as a United Nations agency), or private groups might prepare and disseminate on request information about the nature and potential of civilian-based defense and other forms of nonviolent sanctions in political crises, including *coups d'état* and foreign invasions, and also as a substitute for guerrilla war against entrenched dictatorships and oppressive systems.

33. *Civilian-based defense for the United States?*

While most analysts expect that civilian-based defense will first be adopted by such small countries as Sweden, Norway, or Denmark, and that military Super Powers, such as the United States or the Soviet Union, are likely to be last, various projects are needed on the relevance and possibilities of civilian-based defense for the U.S. and other large countries.

Analysis would be needed of the variety of defense and military-related needs, present, unacknowledged, and future. Not only would obvious differences between defense and offense capacity need analysis and separation, but also separation of the defense of the United States itself from defense measures for other countries. Exploration of the possible role of civilian-based defense in making smaller countries self-sufficient in defense capacity, when they are unable to achieve that by military means is needed; U.S. aid and know-how on civilian-based defense for those countries should be explored. What would be the impact on U.S. defense and military needs if self-defense capacity were restored to all countries which might be threatened by domestic usurpation of foreign invasion?

What would be the defense needs of the United States itself, and to what degree could civilian-based defense meet them? What about the claims that much of U.S. military capacity exists not to defend the country and people, but to defend overseas imperialist economic interests and to support and extend power interests of the U.S. government in diverse parts of the world? What validity is in those charges? How does this affect civilian-based defense, which has a more limited, defensive, capacity? If the charges be true, what would be the impact on present policies if the citizenry became convinced that civilian-based defense was effective for genuine defense needs of the United States itself?

How can the special problems of nuclear weapons be handled, and how would this affect the program for the transarmament (change-over) period. Are large countries, such as the U.S., easier or more difficult than small ones to defend by this civilian policy? What types of internal defense requirements would Americans need to prepare to meet? What economic programs might be required for the phasing out of war industry, for job re-training, for new domestic or overseas programs that might accompany or follow adoption of civilian defense? Again, these are only illustrative of the many problems requiring examination.

THE TECHNIQUE
OF NONVIOLENT ACTION

A. Documentary Studies

34. *A catalog of cases of nonviolent action:*

This project would compile as complete a listing as possible of cases of socially or politically significant nonviolent action and of predominantly nonviolent struggles, along with certain standard information about the cases, with bibliographical sources and research clues. Such data as the following might be included: the groups involved, the nature and status of each group; the issue at conflict (specific and general); dates and place of the conflict; motivation for selection of nonviolent behavior; specific methods of action used (as social boycott, civil disobedience, etc.); opponent's methods of repression and/or reaction; results of the struggle. If a typology of nonviolent action conflict situations has by then been developed, the case could be catalogued accordingly. It might be desirable to have a system of cross-filing under the various listed qualities of the struggle to facilitate comparative analysis.

Among the possible uses of such a catalogue are the following:

A. A catalogue of nonviolent cases would make possible the selection of the most relevant cases for study in examining 1) the validity of hypotheses and claims made by proponents and critics concerning the applicability of such methods; 2) the significance of a number of variables operating in nonviolent action as these affect the processes and outcome of the struggle.

B. Such a catalogue would be of considerable assistance in the study of the cultural, political, religious, and other conditions under which this technique has been previously applied.

C. It would provide a means of compiling research clues and bibliographies which may be of cosiderable assistance later to researchers preparing documentary accounts and analyses of such cases.

The compiling of such material could be divided, roughly, into: 1) historical cases, which would involve library research and consultation with individuals and groups with specialized knowledge; and 2) contemporary cases, involving constant scanning of selected periodicals and communication with persons and groups in various parts of the world who are likely to have such information. This project would be a continuing one, new revisions of the catalogue and new information being issued from time to time.

35. Detailed multi-factor computer catalogue of cases:

In addition to the research-oriented catalogue of cases, a very different, much more detailed catalogue is needed which would contain information for each case on a large number of standard factors and variables, as complete as possible. This could probably only be done on the basis of detailed case studies as discussed below. This catalogue should be constructed with the use of a computer in mind, which would make the vast amount of material both accessible and manipulable. This would assist in a variety of types of analysis, such as factors which may be common to cases of "success," "failure," and intermediary results. Among the variety of studies which might be made possible with such computer-aided analyses would be the testing of hypotheses by inserting variables into known situations, and constructing situations in order to test hypotheses.

36. *Historical documentary studies of cases of nonviolent action:*

There are far too few detailed documentary accounts of past nonviolent action. Generally speaking there has been little effort to learn from past cases with a view to increasing our general understanding of the nature of this technique, and to gaining particular knowledge which might be useful in future struggles and might contribute to increased substitution of nonviolent action for violence. Study of past cases of nonviolent action and of predominantly nonviolent struggles could provide the basis for a more informed assessment of the future political potentialities of the technique. Detailed documentary accounts can also provide material for analyses of particular facets of the technique and help in the formulation of hypotheses which might be tested in other situations. Preparation of detailed documentary accounts of a large number of specific cases is therefore needed, accompanied if possible by separate collections of existing interpretations and explanations of the events.

From these accounts can be learned, for example, in exactly what kind of situation the technique was used, how it was applied in particular cases, how the actionists and population behaved, how the opponent reacted, what types of repression were imposed, how the actionists and population responded to the repression, how volunteers were obtained, the actionists and population disciplined and organized, and many other aspects.

The accounts need to be as detailed and thorough as is reasonably possible in order to fulfill effectively both the educative function of enabling the reader to learn directly from the past events and also to serve as good bases for analyses and evaluations.

It is important that these studies be as objective as possible, be both intensive and extensive in their coverage, and be written in a factual, descriptive, and readable style. They obviously must be scholarly.

Cases for detailed research may be selected on the basis of such criteria as: 1) the estimated present significance of the case for increasing knowledge, 2) special or unusual characteristics of the case, and 3) the availability of resources, research workers, and historical material. Among the cases which may be particularly relevant are the following: the Russian 1905 Revolution and the February 1917 Revolution; resistance to the 1920 Kapp *Putsch* in Germany; resistance to the 1923 French and Belgian occupation of the Ruhr; the 1930-1931 independence campaign in India; Hungarian passive resistance against Austrian rule from 1850-1867; the Moslem

"Servants of God" nonviolence movement among the Pathans in the Northwest Frontier Province of British India, led by Khan Abdul Ghaffar Khan; the defeated 1919-1922 Korean symbolic nonviolent protest against Japanese rule; cases where nonviolent action was later abandoned for violence (Nagaland, Tibet, South Africa and others); Latin American nonviolent "civilian insurrections" against dictators (El Salvador and Guatemala in 1944 and Haiti in 1956); the "bloodless revolution" against General Aboud's regime in the Sudan in December 1964-January 1965; resistance in Nazi-occupied countries during World War II; efforts by non-cooperation, obstruction, and demonstrations to save Jews from the Nazi-extermination program; resistance, risings, and revolution in Communist countries (East Germany 1953, Soviet prison camps 1953, Hungary 1956); Czechoslovak national resistance to invasion and occupation August 1968 through 1969; the undermining of the Shah's regime in Iran in 1978-1979; and Poland, from 1980, during the struggles of Solidarity both for democratization and against martial law.

37. Documentary studies of nonviolent action in American history:

Although obviously not excluded from comprehensive accounts, examples of nonviolent action in American history could be of special interest to American scholars and public, and of importance in possible future practice within this country. Contrary to popular impressions, there exists a vast American history of nonviolent struggles, including colonial struggles before April 1775, international economic sanctions employed by Presidents Jefferson and Madison instead of war, nonviolent abolitionist actions, strikes, economic boycotts by the labor movement, anti-war activities, the civil rights movement, and a large number of others. All of these need to be studied in detail and their roles in United State history evaluated. Revisions may be needed in the overall view of the roles of various types of struggle in the development of the United States and in assumptions about the necessity of violence in earlier major conflicts.

38. Case studies of nonviolent action - guerilla warfare mixes:

Several serious strategists have proposed that civilian-based defense measures would be more effective if combined with guerrilla warfare, terrorism, or other violent resistance. In addition to other projects directly relevant to this problem, it would be of considerable assistance to have case studies of instances in which such a combination happened or was attempted. These would then need to be analyzed in terms of the special ways in which nonviolent action works, and in terms of particular civilian-based defense problems.

39. *Simultaneous research on current struggles:*

Also highly important is the preparation of documentary accounts while a nonviolent campaign is proceeding. These may, at times, suffer from unavailability of secret government reports or private records, etc., which might only be available to the public some years or decades later. But this disadvantage would be offset by being able to gather day-by-day detailed information and clues which might otherwise never be recorded; the principal participants would be lost forever. These accounts would be case studies of contemporary social history, drawing upon as much material as possible while the events take place and recording clues to be followed up at a later point. The researchers would thus be producing from original sources data which might otherwise never be recorded, the principal participants would be available for questioning, and the kind of data which has a way of disappearing could be noted. Hypotheses as to the possible course of events and the processes involved could be noted. This phase of study merges into analysis which might or might not be combined with this. In addition to the descriptive accounts, the team of researchers could prepare analyses of the course of events. This type of project for cases of nonviolent action is very similar to that launched in past years by the Carnegie Endowment for International Peace on instances of interstate conflict.

These on-the-spot research projects depend in part on geographical proximity of potential researchers to current or new cases of nonviolent action, on financial resources, and on the quality and number of research workers available.

B. The operation of nonviolent action

40. *The methods of nonviolent action:*

Further attention is needed to the study of the specific methods or forms of nonviolent action (such as *particular* types of political noncooperation, strikes, boycotts, etc.). Detailed studies are needed of the specific methods and the broad classes of methods, particularly studies using comparative historical material which might shed light on such questions as the conditions in which particular methods may be most applicable and successful, the possible necessity of combining different types of methods, whether the methods used in a given case really influence the power relationships of the contending groups or whether they are largely symbolic and psychological in their impact. These are only illustrative. Further studies might be directed to determining whether deliberate efforts could increase the effectiveness of methods which in the past have not proved outstandingly effective, and to exploring the possible influence of such factors as advance preparations and training. Attention should also be focussed on discovering other methods, existing methods still largely unknown or new methods evolved in the course of actual struggles, or produced by original thought.

41. *Dynamics and mechanisms of change in nonviolent action:*

More detailed research is required on the dynamics of the course of struggle in nonviolent action, and on the mechanisms of change which operate in this technique, as distinct from other types of struggle. Case studies are likely to shed light on how these processes and forces operate, and the conditions in which the mechanisms of conversion, accommodation, and nonviolent coercion operate. Various hypotheses on the dynamics and mechanisms of this technique are implicit or explicit in the literature. They need to be tested, and new ones developed and subjected also to research. These studies may illuminate the complicated processes of change involved in this type of struggle and the conditions under which successful results are likely.

42. *Empirical research on current conflicts:*

Various types of polls, questionnaires and interviews may be used to measure responses to nonviolent action in changes in attitudes, opinions, hostility and the like both among the target group and the general public. Such research might be conducted independently of the action group, in cooperation with it, and (rarely) even by the group itself, though problems of bias may then occur.

43. *Testing response to violent and nonviolent behavior:*

Psychological experiments and tests, as well as careful examination of past experiences, may shed some factual light on the question of the types of responses which may be expected to lead to violence, nonviolent action, and passivity. Various extant assumptions need to be tested, such as the assumption that, when faced with violent behavior, only the threat or use of superior violence will halt the original violence ("The only thing they understand is brute force."). Others that need to be tested are: that violent behavior tends to provoke a violent response which tends in turn to provoke further violence; that nonviolent behavior similarly tends to induce nonviolent behavior in response; that repeated nonviolent responses to violence tend to reduce or eliminate the violence; that an absence of strong resistance to aggressive behavior tends to reinforce such aggression and violence. It is desirable to have empirical data on these and comparable assumptions, including the conditions and possible time-lags under which they may operate.

44. *Political power, its sources and relationship to the population:*

Examination is needed on the nature of political power over large groups of people, its sources, whether (as theorists of nonviolent action maintain) such power depends upon cooperation from the ruled, and whether its withdrawal therefore may threaten the regime. Careful attention is required into such problems as whose cooperation, of what types, and at which times, are most important, and of the roles and limits of repression and other controls for inducing maintenance or resumption of obedience and cooperation.

45. *Studies of violent struggle:*

Not only is it important to understand the nature of violent types of struggle for their own sake, but special studies of such violence are needed to shed light on the ways in which they may both be similar to, and differ from, nonviolent struggle. This general formulation needs to be broken down into specifics. For example, in which ways are guerrilla warfare and nonviolent action similar and dissimilar in their assumptions and dynamics? What can be learned both positively and negatively from studies of military strategy which may be useful in nonviolent strategy? What similar, or (more likely) differing, impacts may violent and nonviolent struggle respectively have on the population and leadership of the opponent group, and also of the struggle group? What similarities and differences may there be in results, short-term and long-term, and side-effects?

The assumptions of the different types of nonviolent action need to be compared with those of different types of violent action, and their respective requirements for effectiveness determined. Specific attention is also needed to the ways in which clashes occur between groups using violent and nonviolent techniques, respectively, and also to the consequences of the introduction of one type of struggle into a conflict predominantly conducted by the other technique.

46. *Means and ends in struggles:*

Efforts are needed to determine how research and critical investigation may be conducted on the possible relationship between the means used in efforts to achieve certain ends, and the ends actually achieved at the conclusion of the effort. What are the relationships between ends and means? Can all, any, or some ends be accomplished by any means? Or, will the use of certain means of action make it impossible to attain the ends which are desired?

What are the factors which have in the past produced results which have differed significantly from the goals espoused at the beginning of the struggle? To what degree can a group seeking to produce social change in fact control the outcome? While philosophical analyses are needed in this field, the most important need is to develop concrete measurements and analyses of social causation on these problems.

47. Analyses of the documentary studies:

The detailed case studies will make possible a series of individual as well as comparative analyses of these struggles, which may shed important light on the nature of nonviolent action. A large number of specific aspects require attention, either individually or as parts of overall analyses. The few questions raised here are only illustrative, and many other possible ones may be derived from other sections of this outline of research areas, from study of the literature on the dynamics of this technique, or from independent thought and analysis.

What role may certain underlying conditions play in making possible the use of this technique? What types of individuals tend to use this technique: responsible, alienated, frustrated, altruistic, or other types? What kinds of groups use this technique against what kinds of opponents, and on what types of issues? Are common characteristics between the contending groups required, and, if so, what are they? What are the roles of the nature of the contending groups, their objectives and perceptions of each other? What are the roles and consequences of the means and modes of combat used by the respective groups: for the nonviolent actionists and specific methods applied, and the tactics, strategy, and grand strategy relied upon, possibly with consideration of unused possible alternatives; for the opponent, the means of repression and other counter-measures used, those available to him but not used (and why), and the consequences of his actions, possibly compared with probable consequences of alternative courses of action? How does the nature of the group acting affect the methods, tactics, and strategy used? How does the group's access to certain types of leverage (say, economic) affect the conflict? How can groups with few or no obvious power leverages in the society use nonviolent action? How is the struggle affected by extreme objectives of the opponent (religious or political conversion, or extermination)? How, in other ways, do the respective belief systems of the contending groups affect the conflict? How do the relative numbers of the two groups influence the context? What is the role of third parties, does it change and why? To what degree does each side achieve its objectives, or are they denied them? Does a comparative analysis of various cases suggest common factors in successful struggles, in defeats, and in those with mixed results? How does the operation of the dynamics and mechanisms differ from one type of situation to another? What were the key factors or decisions, or actions which determined the outcome? Are revisions necessary in existing theories and hypotheses? How do longer-term consequences differ from case to case, and why?

48. *The nature and meaning of success in nonviolent action and other techniques:*

The varying meanings of the terms "success" and "defeat" need to be distinguished, and consideration given to concrete achievements in particular struggles. This careful examination has rarely been made for violent struggles, the victor and vanquished being assumed to be clear. But if the objectives of each side in the conflict are examined in this context, the matter is much more complex than may at first appear. One or more systems of criteria by which to measure success and defeat in all conflicts, using diverse techniques of action, may therefore be necessary, as well, perhaps, as criteria for such measurement with individual techniques of struggle.

Within the context of civilian-based defense, as with other defense systems, there appear to be varying degrees of success and defeat which need to be distinguished if the struggles are to be evaluated intelligently and alternative courses of action wisely determined at each stage. A very limited success, for example, if interpreted either as a full success, or as a total failure, may lead to disastrous strategic decisions. For example, failure within a short period of time to get an invader to withdraw fully from an occupied country may nevertheless be accompanied by the frustration of several of the invader's objectives, the maintenance of a considerable degree of autonomy within the occupied country, and the initiation of a variety of changes in the invader's own regime and homeland which may themselves later lead either to the desired full withdrawal, or to further relaxation of occupation rule. With various types of "success" or "defeat" distinguished, it would be highly desirable to have a study of the various conditions under which they have occurred in the past and seem possible in the future. These conditions would include factors in the social and political situation, the nature of the issues in the conflict, the type of opponent and his repression, the type of group using nonviolent action, the type of nonviolent action used (taking into account quality, extent, strategy, tactics, methods, persistence in face of repression, etc.), and, last, the possible role and influence of "third parties."

INTERNAL USES OF
NONVIOLENT ACTION

Most of the history of nonviolent action has been in conflicts within a country, on issues which did not directly involve defense of the legitimate government. Such cases are likely to be important also in the future. While they are not dependent upon adoption of civilian-based defense, satisfactory experience in their use in place of internal violence — substantiating basic assumptions of the nonviolent technique — would be a contribution to the preparation of the population for civilian-based defense against more formidable opponents. Conversely, unsatisfactory domestic experience may make people skeptical about more ambitious plans. Many people may be interested in these uses of nonviolent action, though indifferent to the needs and claims for civilian-based defense.

A large variety of problems are involved within this general field of internal conflict. They have to do not only with the question of how nonviolent action may be used effectively for a variety of particularly internal objectives, but also with the relationship of such action to the society as a whole, with the impact on social order and the present or alternate systems of government, with the consequences of the use of these forms of action for objectives which many regard as reactionary and anti-social, and with the broader question of whether or not, in one selected area after another, violent sanctions within the society might progressively be replaced with nonviolent ones.

The problems in this area will obviously vary from country to country, and with social, economic and political conditions. A country where a high degree of social justice and democratic controls exist will obviously differ vastly in the roles for nonviolent action from another where a home-grown dictator rules, or where vast inequities in ownership and control of wealth condemn millions to poverty. The intent here is simply to list some of the areas in which investigations of the potential roles and problems of nonviolent alternatives are needed. The problems here are grouped into three broad classes.

49. *Protest, reform and single issues:*

Nonviolent action may be applied by small or large groups to achieve some limited objective. A particular policy of a private institution or the government may arouse dissent and protest which is expressed by use of this technique. Minority and even larger groups, racial, religious, political, sexual, ethnic, and the like may be, or believe themselves to be, discriminated against or denied certain basic liberties which they believe themselves to be entitled to, and hence may resort to nonviolent action to obtain them. Other particular conditions may be seen as injustices to some group; administrative policies and practices may arouse others to act in this manner. In still other cases, people who do not reject military defense as such may use nonviolent action to oppose a particular war and to attempt to bring it to a halt.

50. *Alteration of power relationships within the society:*

In other types of situations, nonviolent struggle may be used for producing major alterations of internal power relationships, or even of revolution. The early use by trade unions of strikes and economic boycotts was certainly not simply for economic improvements, but also for changes in the power relationships between private industry and the factory workers; consequently union recognition and political rights, such as universal manhood suffrage, were important objectives. Where an internal dictatorship rules, an objective of nonviolent action has on several occasions been its disintegration and destruction. Nonviolent action also has potential which has not been fully developed for altering the ownership and control of aspects of the economy, especially where these are highly concentrated in the hands of a minority of wealthy people while most people live in poverty. Land reform, and increased participation in, or transfer of, ownership and control of the economy are also included here.

51. *Maintenance of order, liberties, and the social system:*

Since nonviolent action may be used to defend, as well as to change conditions, nonviolent action may be used in various and even conflicting ways. Such methods may be used, for example, against government policies and even against other nonviolent action in order to resist social changes and to prevent progressive improvements in the society. Nonviolent action has also been used to defend the existing social system against efforts of a foreign-aided dictatorial group to remake it according to ideological preconceptions. Attention is also needed to various efforts and proposals to deliberately replace violence with nonviolent action in dealing with various groups within the society (for example the mentally ill, prisoners, juvenile delinquents, suspected criminals); to whether nonviolent sanctions might be developed as enforcements of particular laws and practices instead of violence and threats of violence; and to how social groups might use nonviolent means of social defense against hostile attacks by other private groups within the society. Examination is also needed of the implications and problems of various groups using nonviolent sanctions against each other in place of either private violence or State violence — would this constitute "creative conflict" or simply produce social disintegration and chaos, leading to greater violence?

Within all three of these areas a large variety of problem-oriented projects can be developed; many other topics are obviously possible. It is important in this area to view such problems from a variety of political perspectives, and to examine the relationship of such direct action to the society itself and the arrangements of its social institutions.

IMPLICATIONS AND CONSEQUENCES OF NONVIOLENT ALTERNATIVES

52. Domestic consequences:

Since civilian-based defense constitutes a direct defense of the society by action of the civilian population and their organizations and institutions, this policy has implications for changes in the society. (Since military defense also seems to have rather different, largely centralizing, influences on the society, it should not be a surprise that this alternate policy may also have certain influences.) The extent and nature of these social consequences require attention. Are they simply decentralization and vitalization of participation in the institutions of the society, or are there other less obvious consequences likely, either good or bad? Are structural changes required or not? What kind of society can be defended by civilian-based defense, and how — with difficulty, with ease, or not at all? This needs to be examined on the basis of historical evidence, not ideological preconceptions. Do efforts to improve the society become, simultaneously then, defense efforts? What are the likely effects on the society of civilian-based defense, in terms of possible increased politicization, and training of the citizenry in methods of nonviolent action?

53. Possible harmful effects:

Objections to the expansion of knowledge about nonviolent struggle have been raised to the effect that this technique will fall into the "wrong hands," and contribute to either advancing disliked causes and objectives or to unjustified social disruption, or to both. Others have answered that one should be grateful that one's political opponents are using nonviolent means instead of violence, and that some social disruption is preferable to both extensive internal violence and to popular passivity in face of grievances and orderly domination by elite groups. In any case, as exponents of this view have argued, the long-term consequences of development of nonviolent alternatives in the society will be beneficial, compared with the alternatives.

Other critics have suggested in relation to civilian-based defense that the degree of organization required and the preparation of capacity for solidarity for future defense struggles will make the society less democratic. They have even suggested that the capacity for preparations, training, and application of nonviolent struggle could be used for internal repression in the "wrong hands." On the other hand, the answer has been offered that the dangers here are minimal, that elites cannot apply nonviolent sanctions without the cooperation of the mass of necessary participants, who may refuse when they do not agree with the purpose of the action.

All these and related considerations of the potential harmful consequences on the society of the possible misuse of nonviolent sanctions require examination.

54. Civilian-based defense and foreign policy:

Under present conditions, as in the past, foreign policy and military defense are usually seen as inter-related, and often highly so. Probably a much closer relationship would exist between civilian-based defense measures and the country's foreign policy. Measures to reduce the prospects of international aggression, to resist the rise and continuation of dictatorships, to gain friends abroad (even within possible enemy countries), and to expand the number of countries relying on civilian-based defense policies, possibly with mutual aid of various types among them, etc., would all require careful advance and continual attention.

55. Civilian-based defense and national and international law:

Civilian-based defense would require a number of changes in the laws of a nation adopting it. These would include not only the acts authorizing its adoption for defense of the country and particular ways for handling the change-over period, but also a whole series of other legal measures, including authorization for various types of preparations, training, research establishments, planning agencies, defense organizations and institutions. Legislation might also be appropriate to deal with the obligation of citizens to participate in training for civilian-based defense, and to defend the country in times of crisis, potentially including certain standards and some types of sanctions against collaboration. In a large country, and especially in a federal system such as the United States, various types of state, provincial, or local legislation would also probably be required.

It is possible that a reformulation or refinement of certain standards of international law might be needed, especially concerning the rights and duties of citizens of occupied countries, the duties of other governments in their relations with an aggressor country, and their duties vis-à-vis the legitimate constitutional government and population of the country which is the victim of international aggression or of internal minority usurpation. These are simply illustrative of legal questions requiring attention.

56. *International reactions to the limited adoption of civilian-based defense:*

Attention is needed to the various possible international consequences of the adoption of civilian-based defense by only one or a few countries, while others maintained their military capacities. One may hypothesize reactions from one extreme to the other, from invasion by an expansive military power regarding this as an invitation to aggression, to the inducement of a rival power, no longer fearing attack, to transarm similarly to civilian-based defense. The real situation, however, would be much more complicated than this implies. It is important to weigh the possibilities of such reactions in order to explore preparations for meeting them; this will also assist in evaluations of the policy itself.

57. *Self-liberation of countries already under tyrannical rule:*

The use of nonviolent struggles in countries already under a domestic or foreign dictatorship does not formally come under "civilian-based defense" which implies *advance* preparations and training in peacetime to meet attempted usurpations. Such self-liberation is, however, related to the defense policy in a number of ways.

1) The changes of international aggression may diminish as a result of the alteration or overthrow of expansionist dictatorships.

2) Military aggression by such a regime against a country with a civilian-based defense policy may, under certain circumstances (according to some exponents of civilian-based defense), lead to a rising in the invader's homeland.

3) In peacetime, preparations in civilian-based defense countries might stimulate liberation groups to apply similar methods and related strategies against their own internal oppressive regime.

All these, and many other related possibilities, and the numerous problems they involve, would require considerable research and analysis.

58. *Consequences of civilian-based defense capacity for international relations:*

Examination needs to be given to at least three aspects of this area. First the development of a country's internal capacity for this type of self-defense may contribute to altering past relationships and forming new ones with a particular country (or countries) which has in the past exercised some form of dominance — even outright occupation — over it. The beginnings of a change in the relationship may rest in large degree on a recognition by the formerly dominant country that the use or threat of military power is no longer capable of achieving domination, and on a recognition by the formerly subordinate country that its self-reliance is basically dependent on nonmilitary factors. The alteration of the relationship between Norway and Sweden (the turning point being the crisis of 1905) may be an instructive case. Today, despite some feelings of hostility, recourse to violence between the countries is virtually inconceivable. Altered relationships between certain ex-colonial powers and their former colonies may also provide insights. In addition to the specific role of capacity for effective struggle, associated social and economic conditions would probably merit attention.

Second, attention should be given to the kind of international relationships which might exist in a world in which one, several, or even many countries had transformed their conventional military or nuclear capacities. This problem requires not only speculation but also careful examination of the variety of influences and forces which might be operative under diverse circumstances.

Third, examination should be made of the possible forms which international relationships and international organizations might take in a world in which many or most countries had transarmed to civilian-based defense. Such an international system would obviously differ not only from that of today, but also from a world government with a monopoly of military power. What would be its characteristics? What are the forms of concerted international action most appropriate for dealing with aggressive military-armed countries, who are either fighting each other or are attacking countries with civilian-based defense policies?

59. *The United Nations and civilian-based defense:*

There are a whole series of possible roles related to civilian-based defense for various branches and agencies of the United Nations and other international organizations. The following are simply suggestive: research and dissemination of information about this defense policy to member countries; international inspection of transarmed civilian-based defense countries to ensure to others that the change-over is genuine; investigation and dissemination of facts when international aggression takes place; condemnation of the aggressor before world opinion; the institution of various types of international political and economic sanctions against the agressor; the launching of various types of help to the attacked civilian-based defense country (such as monetary aid, supplies, broadcasting facilities, continued recognition only of its legitimate government, etc.); and possible action by certain types of U.N. forces intervening in the situation.

It is also possible that the United Nations might play a role if civilian-based defense were adopted simultaneously by several countries in a coordinated and phased program of transarmament, say, on a continental basis or as a part of a program of tension-reduction and demilitarization in certain areas. Various other roles might exist for the United Nations in relation to civilian-based defense. But any effective U.N. support would require advance examination and planning. The research possibilities are numerous.

THE AUTHOR

Gene Sharp, D. Phil. (Oxon), is Program Director, Program on Nonviolent Sanctions, Center for International Affairs, Harvard University, and Professor of Political Science and Sociology at Southeastern Massachusetts University. He is also president of the Albert Einstein Institution for Nonviolent Alternatives in Conflict and Defense.

His books include: *The Politics of Nonviolent Action* (1973), *Gandhi as a Political Strategist* (1979), *Social Power and Political Freedom* (1980), and *Making Europe Unconquerable* (1985). His writings have been translated into several languages.

Dr. Sharp is an international lecturer, and has spoken widely on American college and university campuses.